*Open Heart, Clear Mind*

# Open Heart, Clear Mind

Thubten Chodron

Foreword by His Holiness the Dalai Lama

Snow Lion Publications
Ithaca, New York USA

Snow Lion Publications
P.O. Box 6843
Ithaca, NY 14851
USA

Printed in the USA

ISBN 0-937938-87-4

**Library of Congress Cataloging-in-Publication Data**

Thubten Chodron, 1950–
    Open Heart, Clear Mind / Thubten Chodron ; Foreword by His
    Holiness the Dalai Lama.
        p.   cm.
    Includes biographical references.
    ISBN 0-937938-87-4 : $9.95
        1. Buddhism—Doctrines.   2. Spiritual life (Buddhism)   I. Title.
BQ4165.T48    1990
294.3—dc20                                                    90-41454
                                                             CIP
PRINTINGS:
First Printing 1990
Second Printing 1991
Third Printing 1992
Fourth Printing 1993
Fifth Printing 1994
Seventh Printing 1995
Eighth Printing 1996
Ninth Printing 1999

# Contents

**THE DALAI LAMA**

# FOREWORD

The teachings of the Buddha have provided solace and comfort to countless people over the last two thousand five hundred years. During this time their influence has been felt largely in Asian countries, although in recent decades interest has grown remarkably throughout the world. Heartening evidence of this is that persons like Ven. Thubten Chodron, who were neither born nor brought up in traditionally Buddhist countries, have been inspired to devote their time and effort to helping others to benefit from Buddhist practice.

I am happy that she has prepared this book, 'Open Heart, Clear Mind' based on her own experience, which conveys a clear understanding of Buddhism as it has been practised by Tibetans, in easily comprehensible language. These teachings are both subtle and profound, but it is very important that they are made accessible in a way that people can actually put them into practice and derive real benefit from them. I am sure this book will achieve this and that it will prove helpful to general readers, especially those who have little previous acquaintance with Buddhism.

February 20, 1990

# Introduction and Overview

During his 1989 visit to the United States, His Holiness the Dalai Lama, the 1989 winner of the Nobel Peace Prize, spoke directly to the heartfelt concern of people in our modern age:

Everyone in our world is interrelated and interdependent. My own personal peace and happiness are my concern. I'm responsible for that. But the happiness and peace of the entire society is everyone's concern. Each of us has the individual responsibility to do what we're capable of to improve our world.

In our century, compassion is a necessity, not a luxury. Humans are social animals and we must live together, whether we like it or not. If we lack kind hearts and compassion for each other, our very existence is threatened. Even if we're going to be selfish, we should be wisely selfish and understand that our personal survival and happiness depends on others. Therefore, kindness and compassion towards them are essential.

Bees and ants have no religion, no education or philosophy, yet they instinctively cooperate with each other. In doing so, they insure the survival of their society and the happiness of each individual in it. Surely we humans, who are more intelligent and sophisticated, can do the same!

Thus, we each have the individual responsibility to help others in whatever way we can. However, we shouldn't expect to change the world instantly. As long as we're not enlightened, our actions to benefit others will be limited. Without inner peace, it is impossible to have world peace. Therefore, we must improve ourselves and at the same time do what we can to help others.

In his talk, His Holiness directly mentions compassion as an essential element in our world. To make our compassion effective, it must be coupled with wisdom. Compassion wishes all others to be free from suffering and confusion; wisdom directly realizes our ultimate and relative natures. These are the essential components of a healthy and happy life, and they are the essence of the spiritual path.

This book is entitled *Open Heart, Clear Mind*. The open heart is sincere compassion and altruism. This heart is complemented and enhanced by concise wisdom—a clear mind. The union of compassion and wisdom brings the full development of human potential, the enlightened state. An open heart and a clear mind are as relevant today as 2,500 years ago, when Shakyamuni Buddha first described the path to actualize them.

I was initially attracted by the Buddha's teachings because they contained clear techniques to effectively deal with situations in daily life. The instructions on how to subdue anger and attachment worked when I tried them. Of course, it takes time to train our minds and we shouldn't expect instant miracles, but as we familiarize ourselves with realistic and compassionate attitudes, situations that used to upset us no longer do so, and our ability to make our lives meaningful for others increases.

The Buddha was a profound philosopher and psychologist whose instructions can empower us to improve our lives. One needn't consider him or herself a Buddhist to practice these techniques. Real spiritual practice goes beyond the pigeon-holes of "isms." As His Holiness the Dalai Lama often says, "Compassion isn't the property of any one religion or belief system."

In the course of teaching Buddhist philosophy, psychology and meditation in many countries, I've frequently been asked to recommend a good book for beginners, one that's easy to understand and explains the essential points of the Buddha's teachings in a way that relates to twentieth-century life. Although there are many excellent books on Buddhism, most don't fit this description. *Open Heart, Clear Mind* is designed to fill this gap. It's written in everyday English, with as few technical or foreign terms as possible. I've tried to explain clearly the topics in Buddhism that newcomers find most interesting, pertinent or confusing.

This book will give you a taste of Buddha's teachings, but it won't give you all the answers. In fact, it's more likely to arouse additional questions. But that's okay, because we grow when we seek answers to our questions.

In Buddhist study, we're not expected to understand everything we're taught immediately. This is different from one aspect of Western education, in which we're supposed to memorize, understand and repeat back what we're taught. In studying the Dharma, the Buddha's teachings, it's assumed that not everything will be clear to us the first time we hear it. Reviewing the same material repeatedly often reveals new meanings. Discussion with friends can also clarify our understanding.

The Buddha talked about our lives and our minds. So this book isn't about abstract philosophy, it's about experience—our experience—and the way to improve it. Thus, it's helpful to think about what you read in terms of your own life and your experiences.

This book is about Buddha's teachings in general, not one particular Buddhist tradition. However, as I've trained principally in Tibetan Buddhism, the format accords with that presentation.

OVERVIEW

Some of you will read this book from beginning to end, others will pick out sections that are of special interest. If you're in the latter group, the chapter titles are explicit and will help you find your areas of interest.

For those of you who read from cover to cover, the sequence of chapters is intended to guide you. First, the Buddhist approach to the search for truth is explained. The second section, "Working with Emotions," describes our daily experiences and gives some new perspectives on it. This contains many practical techniques for improving our relationships with people.

The third section, "Our Current Situation," looks at our lives from another perspective by introducing the subjects of rebirth and karma. Having understood our current situation, we'll examine our potential for growth—our innate goodness and our precious human life—in the fourth section.

Section five explains how to develop our potential by following the path to enlightenment. The Four Noble Truths was the first teaching the Buddha gave. When we understand the disadvantages of our current situation and our amazing potential, the determination to be free from all unsatisfactory conditions in life will grow within us. This will lead us to practice ethics in order to establish a firm foundation for our future development. From there, we can expand our perspective and recognize others' kindness, thus developing our love, compassion and an altruistic intention. To fulfill our potential and be able to be of greater service to others, we must have wisdom, particularly wisdom of the ultimate nature of existence. Compassion, altruism and wisdom lead us to open hearts and clear minds.

All of these topics provide food for meditation, so meditation is discussed next. Having a general overview of the path to enlightenment, we can then appreciate the qualities of the Buddhas (enlightened beings), the Dharma (spiritual realizations and teachings), and the Sangha (those who help us on the path). This is explained in the chapter on taking refuge.

Some of you may be interested in the life of Shakyamuni Buddha, the founder of the Buddhist philosophy and psychology. The sixth section discusses this and also explains some of the principal Buddhist traditions practiced today. "Compassion in Action" suggests practical ways to implement the Buddha's teachings in our daily lives.

My aim is to give you access to the essence of the Buddha's teachings. Thus, much material has been condensed into a few pages. I have tried give you enough, yet not too much. However, since each person has a different appetite, this is difficult to do! If you seek more information, please read other books, attend Buddhist talks or talk with Buddhist practitioners. I welcome you also to write to me. There is a brief list of resources at the end of the book.

A few linguistic and stylistic points must be mentioned. First, in Buddhist terminology, no difference is made between heart and mind, one word being used for both. For convenience sake, "mind" is used here, although this term doesn't refer to our brain or to our intellect only. Our mind is what perceives and experiences our external and internal worlds. It's formless, and includes our sense consciousnesses, mental consciousness, emotions, intelligence and so on. This will be explained later.

Second, "the Buddha" refers to Shakyamuni Buddha who lived 2,500 years ago in India. However, there are many beings who have attained enlightenment and become Buddhas.

Third, "he/she" and "s/he" are awkward to use for the indefinite third person pronoun. Instead, I use the pronouns "he," "she" and "he or she" interchangeably .

Finally, some words may be unfamiliar or have a somewhat different meaning than in regular usage. A short glossary of Buddhist terms is provided at the back of this book to help you.

## ACKNOWLEDGEMENTS

My heartfelt thanks go to many people who enabled me to write this book. My gratitude to all of my teachers—especially His Holiness the Dalai Lama, Tsenzhab Serkong Rinpoche and Zopa Rinpoche—can't be expressed. The inspiration for writing this book came from students in Singapore and from the people who attended my talks during a lecture tour in the U.S.A. and Canada. Support came from many kind benefactors who fed and housed me, in particular Amitabha Buddhist Center in Singapore, Osel Shenpen Ling in Montana and Dharma Friendship Foundation in Seattle. Special thanks go to Steve Wilhelm and Cindy Loth for editing the manuscript, to Lesley Lockwood and Gary Loth for reviewing it and making valuable suggestions, and to Geshe Thupten Jinpa for checking the difficult sections. The drawings were done by Sonam Jigme and Jangchub Ngawang.

Although I have little understanding of the path to enlightenment, I've tried to repeat here what my kind teachers have taught me. All mistakes are my own.

# PART I

# THE BUDDHIST APPROACH

# The Buddhist Approach

*The fundamental teachings of Gautama (Buddha), as it is now being made plain to us by study of original sources, is clear and simple and in the closest harmony with modern ideas. It is beyond all dispute the achievement of one of the most penetrating intelligences the world has ever known.*

—*H. G. Wells, British historian and writer*

During the introduction to the first Buddhist course I attended, the teacher said, "The Buddha instructed his disciples, 'Do not accept my teachings merely out of respect for me, but analyze and check them the way that a goldsmith analyzes gold, by rubbing, cutting and melting it.' You are intelligent people and should think about what you hear during this course. Don't accept it blindly."

I relaxed. "Good," I thought, "No one will pressure me to believe anything or ostracize me if I don't." During the course, we were encouraged to discuss and debate the topics. I appreciated this approach, for it accorded with my propensity to analyze and explore issues from various viewpoints.

This is the Buddhist approach. Our intelligence is respected and encouraged. There is no dogma to follow blindly. In fact, we are free to choose whichever of the Buddha's teachings suit us now, and leave the rest aside for the time being, without criticizing them. The Buddha's teachings are similar to a huge buffet dinner. We may like one dish, someone else may enjoy another. There is no obligation to eat everything, nor must we choose what our friend chooses.

Likewise, one subject or meditation technique in the Buddha's teachings may appeal to us, while another may be important to our friend. We should learn and practice according to our own ability at the present moment, so that we improve the quality of our lives. In this way, we'll gradually come to understand and appreciate teachings that seemed difficult or unimportant to us initially.

This open approach is possible because the Buddha described our human experience and how to improve it. He didn't create our situation, nor did he invent the path to enlightenment. He discussed our experience, the workings of our minds, and realistic and practical ways to deal with daily problems. Describing our difficulties and their causes, the Buddha also explained the way to eliminate them. He told of our great human potential and how to develop it. It's up to us to ascertain through logic and our own experience the truth of what he taught. In this way, our beliefs will be well-founded and stable.

Buddhism centers not so much upon the Buddha as a person, or his followers, the Sangha, as upon the Dharma, the teachings and realizations. Shakyamuni Buddha, who lived 2,500 years ago in India, wasn't always a fully enlightened being. He was once an ordinary person like us, with the same problems and doubts we have. By following the path to enlightenment, he became a Buddha.

Similarly, each of us has the ability to become fully compassionate, wise and skillful. The gap between the Buddha and us isn't unbridgeable, for we too can become Buddhas. When we create the causes of enlightenment by accumulating positive potential and wisdom, then we'll automatically become enlightened. Many beings have already done this. Although we often speak of the Buddha, referring to Shakyamuni Buddha, in fact there are many enlightened beings.

Shakyamuni Buddha is respected because he purified his mindstream of every obscuration and developed his good qualities to their fullest extent. The Buddha has done what we aspire to do, and his teachings, as outlined in this book, show us the path to overcome our limitations and develop our full potential. He has offered his wisdom to us and we are free to accept it or not. The Buddha doesn't demand our faith and allegiance, nor are we condemned if we hold different views.

The Buddha advised us to be very practical and to the point, without getting distracted by useless speculation. He gave the example of a man wounded by a poisoned arrow. If, before consenting to have the arrow removed, the man insisted on knowing the name and occupation of the person who shot it, the brand of the arrow, the site where it was manufactured and what type of bow was used, he would die before learning the answers. The crucial thing for him is to treat the present wound and prevent further complications.

Similarly, while we're entangled in the cycle of our physical and mental problems, if we get side-tracked by useless intellectual speculation about irrelevant subjects that we can't possibly answer now, we're foolish. It's far wiser to get on with what's important.

To overcome our limitations and develop our inner beauty, there is a step-by-step process to follow. First we listen or read in order to learn a subject. Then we reflect and think about it. We use logic to analyze it, and examine how it corresponds with our own experiences in life and with what we see in the lives of people around us. Finally, we integrate this new understanding into our being, so that it becomes part of us.

The essence of Buddha's teachings is simple and can be practiced in our daily lives: we should help others as much as possible, and when that isn't possible, we should avoid harming them.

This is compassion and wisdom. This is common sense. It's not mystical or magical, nor is it irrational or dogmatic. All of the Buddha's teachings are geared to enable us to develop wisdom and compassion and integrate them into our daily lives. Common sense isn't just discussed intellectually, it's lived.

The Buddha's teachings are called "the middle way" be-caue they are free from extremes. Just as self-indulgence is an extreme, so is self-mortification. The purpose of the Dharma is to help us relax and enjoy life, although this isn't in the usual sense of sleeping and going to parties. We learn how to relax destructive emotions and attitudes that prevent us from being happy. We understand how to enjoy life without clinging, obsession and worry.

There is an old idea that to be religious or "holy" we must deny ourselves happiness. That is incorrect. Everyone wants to be happy, and it would be wonderful if we all were. But, it's helpful if we understand what happiness is and what it isn't.

In Buddhism we learn about the various types of happiness we're capable of experiencing. We then search for the causes of true happiness, so we can ensure that our efforts will bring the result we desire. Finally, we create the causes for happiness. Happiness—and misery as well—don't come our way by chance or by accident, nor are they due to our placating some higher being. As does everything in the universe, happiness arises due to specific causes. If we create the causes for happiness, the resultant happiness will come. This is a systematic process of cause and effect that will be explained in later chapters.

The goal in Buddhism is simplicity, clarity and spontaneity. A person with these qualities is extraordinary. With simplicity, we leave behind hypocrisy and selfishness, thus letting impartial love and compassion grow in our minds. With clarity we abandon the confusion of ignorance, replacing it with direct perception of reality. With spontaneity, we no longer are influenced by impulsive thoughts, but naturally know the most appropriate and effective ways to benefit others in any situation.

By developing wisdom and compassion, we'll be more content and will know what's important in our lives. Instead of battling the world with a dissatisfied mind that continually wants more and better, we'll transform our attitude so that whatever environment we're in, we'll be happy and will be able to make our lives meaningful.

Some people think that Buddhism teaches passivity and withdrawal from other people. This is not the correct understanding of the Buddha's teachings. Although it's advantageous to distance ourselves from wrong conceptions and misdirected emotions, that doesn't mean we live without energy and purpose. In fact, it's the opposite! Free from confusion, we'll be brighter and more alert. We'll genuinely care about others. Although we'll be able to accept whatever situations we encounter, we'll actively work to benefit those around us.

## THREE FAULTY POTS

The Buddha used the analogy of three faulty pots to explain how to remove obstructions to learning. The first pot is upside-down. Nothing can be poured inside it. This is analogous to reading Dharma books while watching television. We're so distracted that very little of what we read goes inside our minds. The second faulty pot has a hole in the bottom. Something may go inside, but it doesn't stay there. We may read the book with attention, but if a friend later asks us what the chapter was about, we can't remember. The third defective pot is dirty. Even if we pour fresh clean milk inside and it stays there, it becomes undrinkable. This is similar to filtering what we read through our own preconceptions and ideas. We won't understand the subject correctly because it has been polluted with our misinterpretations.

It may be difficult to set aside our preconceptions, because sometimes we aren't aware that our ideas are prejudiced. One suggestion is to try to understand each topic in its own context, without re-interpreting it so it fits into another system we've already learned. In this way, we'll view it freshly, with an open mind. When we have understood the Dharma well in its own context, then we'll be more successful in seeing how it corresponds with psychology, science, or another philosophy or religion.

This book isn't written by a scholar for a group of intellectuals, but as one person sharing with another. We'll explore not only what the Buddha taught but also how it applies to our lives. To do this, we needn't call ourselves "Buddhists," for the search for happiness through living a meaningful life is universal. We'll try to look at our lives with common sense and clarity, as human beings seeking happiness and wisdom. This is the Buddhist approach.

# PART II

# WORKING EFFECTIVELY WITH EMOTIONS

# 1 *Where Is Happiness:*
## Looking closely at our experience

Buddhism describes our problems and sufferings, their causes, the path to liberate ourselves from them, and the resultant state of bliss from having ceased all undesirable experiences. Buddhism is an approach to life that helps us to act effectively and compassionately. It contains practical techniques which can remedy our disturbing attitudes and daily problems.

In the course of one day, we experience many emotions. Some emotions, such as genuine love and compassion, are valuable. Others, attachment, anger, closed-mindedness, pride and jealousy, disturb our mental peace and make us act in ways that disturb others. The chapters in this section will examine these disturbing attitudes and explore some antidotes to pacify and transform them.

All disturbing attitudes are based upon the innate assumption that happiness and pain come from outside of us. It seems that other people and things make us happy or miserable. Thus, we rely on external objects that we contact through our five senses—seeing, hearing, smelling, tasting, touching—to make us happy. We have the notion that happiness is located "out there," in that object, place or person. Consequently, we try to procure certain things and be near certain people. Simi-

larly, we try to avoid all objects and people that make us unhappy, because it appears our unhappiness is coming from
them.

The view that happiness and unhappiness come from external things and people puts us in a predicament, because
we can never completely control the people and things around
us. We try to obtain the possessions we want, but we never
have enough. Continuously disappointed, we search for more
and better of whatever it is we think will bring us happiness.
But do we know one rich person who is totally satisfied? Do
we know one person who is completely content with his friends
and relatives?

Likewise, we think that whenever we have a problem, it's
due to an external person or thing. We attribute our emotional
problems to the way our parents treated us when we were
young. We blame our present dissatisfaction on our employers,
employees, relatives or teachers. We wish that the people
around us would learn to treat us better. Others aren't what
we want them to be, and we are constantly frustrated in our
attempts to make them change.

Our lives can become very complicated as we try to make
the world be what we want it to be. Unfortunately, the world
doesn't cooperate! Our plans and dreams are only partially actualized, if at all. Although we may temporarily succeed in
influencing others' actions, we can't dictate what they feel and
think. When we do get what we want, we're ecstatic; when
we don't, we're disappointed and depressed. Like emotional
yo-yos, we go up and down according to whatever person or
object we meet. We need only look at the number of moods
we've had today to confirm this.

However, once we check our daily life experiences we'll find
that happiness and goodness don't exist in external objects and
people, nor do unhappiness and unpleasantness. If they did
then all of us should perceive and react to things in the same
way, since we'd be perceiving what is "out there," independent of ourselves.

But we don't all like the same people or things: one person

likes pop music while another doesn't. Nor do we always enjoy something: as youngsters we liked comic books, but as adults we may find them boring. This shows that our experiences with people or things depend on our way of viewing and relating to them.

Thus, by changing our interpretations and the way in which we relate to things and people, we can change our experience of them. We can recognize our projections, over- and underestimations of things and people, and then correct these misconceptions. In this way we'll relate to things more realistically and will be more satisfied. By abandoning the misconceptions that lead to attachment, anger, closed-mindedness, pride and jealousy, we'll relate to other people and to possessions in a more balanced way.

## 2  *Taking the Ache Out of Attachment:*
Leading a balanced life


Do you know anyone who is satisfied with what he or she has?
Most people aren't: they would like to have more money, go
on better vacations, buy more things for their homes and have
more attractive clothing. Some people become miserable when
they can't afford the things they want, or even if they have
them they worry about paying the bills at the end of the month.
They're attached to their possessions and are sad when a treas-
ured gift is lost or a family heirloom is broken.

During the day our attention is generally directed outwards.
From morning till night we crave to see beautiful forms, hear
pleasant sounds, enjoy fragrant scents, taste good food and
touch pleasing objects. When we do, we're happy; when we
don't, or when we contact unpleasant sights, sounds, smells,
tastes and tangibles, we're upset. Our feelings and moods go
up and down each day, depending on whether we like or dislike the sense objects we contact.

Although we derive pleasure from sense objects, it's limited
pleasure. If we examine our lives closely, we'll find that what
brings us pleasure at one time makes us unhappy at another.
For example, food is enjoyable when we begin eating, but it's
not when we overeat. Money enables us to have many things,

but it also causes us to worry, because we fear it will be stolen or lost. The things we're attached to don't consistently bring us pleasure.

At the moment, it may seem to us that sensual pleasures are fantastic, but in fact we're capable of greater happiness. According to Buddhism all beings should have pleasure and be happy. However, we must examine closely what happiness is and what causes it. There are many levels of happiness, the pleasures of the senses being one of them. However, we're capable of greater happiness than that experienced by being near beautiful objects and wonderful people. Buddhism directs us towards supreme happiness, which comes from transforming our minds.

The Buddha observed that when we're attached to sense objects, we eventually become unhappy. The problem isn't in the objects, it's in our way of relating to them. How does attachment work? Is it an accurate or necessary way of relating to the people and things in our environment?

Attachment is an attitude that overestimates the qualities of an object or person and then clings to it. In other words, we project onto people and things qualities they don't have, or exaggerate what they do have. Attachment is an unrealistic view and thus causes us confusion.

Let's take food as an example, since it's something most of us are attached to. When we smell or see something tasty, we desire it. It appears to us as if happiness exists inside the food. We feel that if we ate that food, we would have happiness. It appears that the deliciousness of the food exists independently of us, as part of the food's intrinsic nature.

Is this appearance correct? If the food were delicious by nature then everyone should like the same food, because we all like what is delicious. If the goodness existed intrinsically in the food, then it should always be delicious. But when the food is left out overnight, it becomes stale and undesirable. While the food previously appeared to us to be intrinsically and permanently delicious and we believed that appearance, the fact that it changed shows the food is neither permanently nor inherently delicious.

If happiness were an inherent quality of food, then the more we ate, the happier we would be. That certainly isn't the case, for when we overeat we feel miserable! If the food contained happiness, then eating the right amount would make us feel eternally satisfied. However, after a few hours we're hungry.

Although the above arguments may seem self-evident, it's important to examine our own experience clearly. We may intellectually understand something without being able to apply it in our daily lives. For example, intellectually we may know that happiness doesn't exist inside food. However, whenever the desire for our favorite food arises, our actual perception and expectation of the food is quite different. By recognizing this contradiction we'll begin to bring our understanding from our heads into our hearts. We'll be better able to live according to what we know is true, rather than what we unthinkingly assume is true.

When we examine our experience, it becomes clear that we overestimated the qualities of the food and then became attached to it. By eliminating these false projections, we can release the clinging.

That doesn't mean that we stop eating. We have to eat to stay alive, but we can have a realistic, balanced view towards food. If we regard it as a medicine to cure hunger and nourish our bodies, we'll eat peacefully and will be satisfied with what we eat. This satisfaction is a real blessing, for we can't always control what food we have. If we're very picky and always want a fantastic meal, we'll have little contentment simply because we can't always get what we like. The Buddha said in the *Dhammapada*,

> Attachment arises from (wrong) conceptions,
> So know them as attachment's root.
> Avoid conceptualizations
> And then attachment will not arise.

Certain basic misconceptions feed our attachment. These are that (1) things, people and relationships don't change; (2)

they can bring us lasting happiness; (3) they are pure; and (4) they have a real, findable essence.

These misconceptions function whenever we're attached to something or someone. To examine them in more depth, we'll use the example of our bodies.

## CHANGE: THE INEVITABILITY OF AGING

Although we intellectually know we won't be young forever, in the back of our minds we innately feel that we will be. Thus, when we look at pictures taken of ourselves years ago we're surprised at how much we've aged. Our hair is grayer, or maybe we don't have as much hair, and our skin isn't as smooth. In spite of all the anti-wrinkle creams, hair colorings, and anti-balding methods we employ, still our bodies get weaker and less attractive, making us worried and unhappy.

In addition, we don't feel quite as young and energetic as we used to. Although we may exercise and consequently have a lot of energy now, when we were younger that energy was naturally there. Now, we can feel our bodies slowing down and we have to work at feeling fit.

Some people get very unhappy at the inevitability of aging. Western culture, with its emphasis on youth and being fit and attractive, sets the stage for discontent and worry. We idolize what we're all in the process of losing—our youth.

If we realistically recognize and accept the changing nature of our bodies, the unhappiness due to aging will subside. Our bodies are getting older as each moment passes, and there's no way to prevent this. We need to contemplate this so we not only understand it intellectually, but accept it in our hearts. If we think about the inevitability of aging while we're young, we won't be so surprised when it happens.

## DO OUR BODIES BRING US LASTING HAPPINESS?

A second misconception about our bodies is that they bring us lasting happiness. We're very attached to being healthy.

Some people pamper their bodies to keep them well, and worry whenever they cough or sneeze. Such attachment to our health is inconvenient for the people around us. It also causes us to be depressed or angry when we get sick, thus delaying our recovery.

Although no one likes getting sick, our bodies are prone to disease. Who do we know who has never been sick? If mentally we can accept the frailty of our bodies, then when illness comes we'll be better able to handle it. Then, even when we're sick, we'll be able to have a happy mind. A good attitude will automatically help us to get better.

## ARE OUR BODIES PURE AND CLEAN?

Another misconception about our bodies is that they're intrinsically pure and attractive. Thus, we're attached to being good-looking. We feel that we're worthwhile when we look good, and we use our looks to attract people to us. We feel people will like us if we have attractive or athletic bodies and will ignore us if we don't.

Although one part of us thinks our bodies are intrinsically pure, our attachment to our looks makes us perpetually dissatisfied with them. We may employ a variety of products, diets and exercises to make our bodies beautiful, but our wishes are never completely fulfilled. Even the most beautiful women and handsome men aren't satisfied with their bodies. We feel that we bulge where we shouldn't bulge or don't bulge where we should. Although others may tell us how attractive or well-built we are, we never feel our bodies are good enough.

But what is the purpose of our human lives? Is it to look beautiful externally, or to improve our minds and open our hearts so we're more beautiful internally? All of us have met people who aren't physically attractive but who radiate internal qualities of patience and openness that draw people to them. Qualities that make people internally beautiful are more important and last longer than physical beauty. But these qualities don't come by accident; they come because people cultivate them. Contemplating this helps us clarify our relationships to our bodies.

Of course, we should try to stay healthy and to dress neatly, but we can do this without attachment. Over-concern about good looks makes us more unhappy. Being very attractive can bring many added problems, as we can see by the lives of many celebrities. If we recognize that having attractive bodies doesn't eliminate our problems or bring us ultimate happiness, we'll let go of clinging to their being beautiful and well-built. We'll then be less self-conscious and more content with what we are. Recognizing that inner beauty is more important, we'll cultivate this and will have more friends because our characters have improved.

## OUR BODIES DON'T HAVE A REAL ESSENCE

The final misconception is that we believe our bodies have a real essence. However, if we examine our bodies carefully we'll find they're only accumulations of atoms. Scientists tell us there is more open space in our bodies than area occupied by atoms. In addition, these atoms are in continuous motion.

Thus, when we seek a solid, unchanging entity to call "my body," we can't find one. There is no static permanent phenomenon we can identify as the body. Also, since what we label "my body" is merely an accumulation of atoms in a particular formation, our bodies aren't inherent entities. Nor are they inherently attractive or ugly.

These four misconceptions—that our bodies are unchanging, bring lasting happiness, are intrinsically pure and have a real, findable essence—exaggerate the qualities of our bodies. This causes us to cling to being perpetually young, healthy and good looking. Such clinging makes us dissatisfied and anxious.

What is another way to relate to our bodies? At first it may seem inconceivable that there is any other way to relate to our bodies besides being attached to them. Yet there is. One way is to think, "I can make my life meaningful by improving my character, helping the people around me and contributing to society. My body is the vehicle enabling me to do this. Therefore I must keep my body healthy and well-groomed, not for my own selfish purposes but to use it for the benefit of others."

This way of thinking may initially seem foreign, but if we habituate ourselves to it, it will become our natural way of thinking. We'll have a more relaxed way of viewing our bodies and will be much happier for it.

## THE WAY TO SATISFACTION

Attachment lays the foundation for dissatisfaction, for no matter how much we have, we always seek more and better. Our society exploits this greed and discontentment, and we're told that last year's fashions are out, last year's appliances are outdated. But few people are able to afford everything they think they're supposed to have. Even if we can buy many things, they later beome old or break, or we have to get more and better possessions because everyone else has them. This can make us continually insecure.

On the other hand if we think, "What I have is good enough," then our minds will be relaxed. This doesn't mean that we never buy new things or that our society shouldn't improve technologically. If we need something or when a new model is more efficient, there's nothing wrong with buying it, provided we can afford it! But whether we succeed in getting something or not, our minds will be relaxed because we'll be content with what we have. The Buddha said:

If you desire every joy,
Completely forsake all attachment.
By forsaking completely all attachment
A most excellent ecstasy is found.

So long as (you) follow attachment
Satisfaction is never found.
Whoever reverses attachment
With wisdom attains satisfaction.

As long as we crave more, better and different things, we'll never be satisfied no matter what we have. On the other hand if we're content with what we have, we can still work to improve things, but our minds will be relaxed. Free from grasping, we can develop economically and technologically for the benefit of everyone.

At first it may be difficult to think in this way because we're in the habit of being attached. The attachment may be so strong that we fear losing the object or person, and we panic. This fear and clinging obscure our good feelings and prevent us from enjoying our relationships and material possessions.

We can eliminate this fear. First, we can recognize that our own minds project the beautiful object or person and that attachment is a mistaken conception. This will make us more realistic. Then we can remember the disadvantages of attachment and abandon it. Instead we can allow our minds to rest in an open state of contentment, knowing that if we have that object or are near that person, it's nice, but if not, we can also be happy.

For some people, the word "detachment" has a negative connotation because it implies being ascetic, apathetic or uncaring. However, this isn't the Buddhist meaning of detachment. Rather, it refers to a balanced state of mind in which we don't grasp at things and therefore are free to focus our attention on what is really worthwhile.

Being detached doesn't mean we give away all of our possessions and live in a cave. There is nothing harmful about having possessions. We need a certain number of them in order to live. Problems arise only when we unrealistically exaggerate the importance of our possessions. Attachment and clinging cause the problems, not the possessions. Being free of attachment we can enjoy things.

When we use our possessions it's helpful to think, "Many people worked to produce the things I enjoy, and I'm grateful to them. Instead of using my possessions with selfish attachment, I'll use them with the aspiration to improve my qualities so I can love and help others more." We can enjoy food, clothes, a home and possessions, but with a different motivation than before. Doing so, we'll be peaceful and free from anxiety.

Nor does leaving aside attachment make us unmotivated and indifferent. At first glance it may seem like this simply because we're very habituated to attachment. However, there is a variety of other attitudes that can motivate us. Genuine care for others is one. The wish to bring others happiness and prevent their suffering can be a powerful motivating force in our lives. Thus, avoiding attachment opens the door to genuine communication with others, love and compassion.

## 3  *Love vs. Attachment:*
### Distinguishing genuine care from unrealistic projections

All of us would like to have positive feelings for others. We know that love is the root of world peace. What is love and how do we develop it? What is the difference between loving people and being attached to them?

Love is the wish for others to be happy and to have the causes of happiness. Having realistically recognized others' kindness as well as their faults, love is focused on others' welfare. We have no ulterior motives to fulfill our self-interest; we love others simply because they exist.

Attachment, on the other hand, exaggerates others' good qualities and makes us crave to be with them. When we're with them, we're happy; when we're separated, we're miserable. Attachment is linked with expectations of what others should be or do.

Is love as it is usually understood in our society really love? Before we know people they are strangers, and we feel indifferent towards them. After we meet them they may become dear ones for whom we have strong emotions. Let's look closer at how people become our friends.

Generally we're attracted to people either because they have qualities we value or because they help us. If we observe our own thought processes, we'll notice that we look for specific qualities in others. Some of these are qualities we find attractive, others are those our parents or society value. We examine someone's looks, education, financial situation and social status. If we value artistic or musical ability, we look for that. If athletic ability is important to us, we check for that. Thus, each of us has different qualities we look for and different standards for evaluating them.

If people have the qualities on our "internal checklist" we value them. We think they're good people who are worthwhile. It appears to us as if they are great people in and of themselves, unrelated to our evaluation of them. But in fact, because we have certain preconceptions about which qualities are desirable and which aren't, we're the ones who create the worthwhile people.

In addition, we judge people as worthwhile according to how they relate to us. If they help us, praise us, make us feel secure, listen to what we say and care for us when we're sick or depressed, we consider them good people. This is very biased, for we judge them only in terms of how they relate to us, as if we were the most important person in the world.

Generally we think that if people help us, they're good people; while if they harm us, they're bad people. If people encourage us, they're wonderful; if they encourage our competitor, they're obnoxious. It isn't their quality of encouragement that we value, but the fact that it's aimed at us. Similarly, if people criticize us, they're mistaken or inconsiderate. If they criticize someone we don't like, they're wise. We don't object to their trait of criticizing, only its being aimed at us.

The process by which we discriminate people isn't based on objective criteria. It's determined by our own preconceptions of what is valuable and how that person relates to us. Underlying this are the assumptions that we're very important and that if people help us and meet our preconceived ideas of goodness then they're wonderful in and of themselves.

After we've judged certain people to be good, whenever we see them it appears to us as if goodness is coming from them. However, were we more aware, we'd recognize that we have projected this goodness onto them.

If certain people were objectively worthwhile and good, then everyone would see them that way. But someone we like is disliked by another person. This occurs because each of us evaluates others based on our own preconceptions and biases. People aren't wonderful in and of themselves, independent of our judgment of them.

Having projected goodness onto some people, we form fixed conceptions of who they are and then become attached to them. Some people appear near-perfect to us and we yearn to be with them. Desiring to be with the people who make us feel good, we become emotional yo-yos: when we're with those people, we're up; when we're not, we're down.

In addition, we form fixed concepts of what our relationships with those people will be and thus have expectations of them. When they don't live up to our expectations we're disappointed or angry. We want them to change so that they will match what we think they are. But our projections and expectations come from our own minds, not from the other people. Our problems arise not because others aren't who we thought they were, but because we mistakenly thought they were something they aren't.

For example, after Jim and Sue were married for a few years, Jim said, "Sue isn't the same woman I married. When we got married she was so supportive and interested in me. She's so different now." What happened?

First, Sue's personality isn't fixed. She's constantly changing in response to the external environment and her internal thoughts and feelings. It's unrealistic to expect her to be the same all the time. All of us grow and change, going through highs and lows.

Second, can we ever assume we know who someone else is? When Jim and Sue were getting to know each other before they were married, each one built up a conception of who the other one was. But that conception was only a conception. It wasn't the other person. Jim's concept of Sue wasn't Sue. However, because Jim wasn't aware of this, he was surprised when different aspects of Sue's personality came out. The stronger his concept of her was, the more he was unhappy when she didn't act according to it.

How strange to think we completely understand another person! We don't even understand ourselves and the changes we go through. We don't understand everything about a speck of dust, let alone about another person. The false conception that believes someone is who we think he or she is makes our lives complicated. On the other hand if we are aware that our concept is only an opinion, then we'll be much more flexible.

For example, parents may form a fixed conception of their teenager's personality and how she should behave. When their child misbehaves, the parents are shocked and a family quarrel ensues. However, if the parents understand that their child is a constantly changing person like themselves, then they won't have such a strong emotional reaction to her behavior. With a calm mind free of expectations the parents can be more effective in helping their maturing child.

When others act in ways which don't correspond with our concepts of them we become disappointed or angry. We may try to cajole them into becoming what we expected. We may nag them, boss them around or try to make them feel guilty. When we do this our relationship deteriorates further, and we're miserable.

The sources of the pain and confusion are our own biased projections and the selfish expectations we've placed on others. These are the foundation of attachment. Attachment overestimates our friends and relatives and clings to them. It opens the door for us to be upset and angry later. When we're separated from our dear ones we're lonely; when they're in a bad mood we resent it. If they fail and don't achieve what we'd counted on we feel betrayed.

To avoid the difficulties caused by attachment we must be aware of how attachment operates. Then we can prevent it by

correcting our false preconceptions of others and not project-
ing new ones. We'll remember that people are constantly changing and they don't have fixed personalities. Recalling that it's
impossible for us always to be with our dear ones, we won't
be so upset when we're separated. Rather than feeling dejected
because we aren't together, we'll rejoice for the time we had
together.

## I LOVE YOU IF...

"Checklist love" isn't love, for it has strings attached. We think,
"I love you if...," and we fill in our requirements. It's difficult for us to sincerely care about others when they must fulfill certain requirements which center around the benefit they
must give to us. In addition, we're often fickle in what qualities and behavior we want from others. One day we want our
dear one to take the initiative; the next day we want him or
her to be dependent.

What we call love is often attachment, a disturbing attitude
that overestimates the qualities of the other person. We then
cling to him or her thinking our happiness depends on that
person. Love, on the other hand, is an open and relaxed attitude. We want someone to be happy simply because he or she
exists.

While attachment is uncontrolled and sentimental, love is
direct and powerful. Attachment obscures our judgment and
we become partial, helping our dear ones and harming those
we don't like. Love clarifies our minds, and we assess a situation by thinking of the greatest good for everyone. Attachment
is based on selfishness, while love is founded upon cherishing
others.

Attachment values others' superficial qualities: their looks,
intelligence, talents, social status and so on. Love looks beyond these superficial appearances and dwells on the fact that
they are just like us: they want happiness and want to avoid
suffering. If we see unattractive, dirty, ignorant people, we feel
repulsed because our selfish minds want to know attractive,

clean and talented people. Love, on the other hand, doesn't evaluate others by these superficial standards and looks deeper. Love recognizes that regardless of others' appearances, their experience is similar to ours: they seek to be happy and to avoid problems.

This is a profound point which determines whether we feel alienated or related to those around us. In public places, we look at those around us and often comment on them to ourselves, "He's too fat, she walks funny, he certainly has a sour expression, she's arrogant." Of course we don't feel close to others when we allow our negative thoughts to pick out their faults.

When we catch ourselves thinking like this, we can pause and then regard the same people through different eyes: "Each one of these people has their own internal experience. Each one only wants to be happy. I know what that's like, because I'm the same way. They all want encouragement, kindness, or even a smile from others. None of them enjoys criticism or disrespect. They're exactly like me!" When we think like this, love arises and instead of feeling distant from others, we feel connected to them.

Attachment makes us possessive of the people we're close to. Someone is MY wife, husband, child, parent. Sometimes we act as if people were our possessions and we were justified in telling them how to live their lives. However, we don't own our dear ones. We don't possess people like we do objects.

Recognizing that we never possess others causes attachment to subside. It opens the door for love, which genuinely treasures every living being. We may still advise others and tell them how their actions influence us, but we respect their integrity as individuals.

## FULFILLING OUR NEEDS

When we're attached we're not emotionally free. We overly depend on and cling to another person to fulfill our emotional needs. We fear losing him or her, feeling we'd be incomplete without our dear one. Our self-concept is based on having a particular relationship: "I am so-and-so's husband, wife, parent, child, etc." Being so dependent, we don't allow ourselves to develop our own qualities. In addition, by being too dependent we set ourselves up for depression, because no relationship can continue forever. We separate when life ends, if not sooner.

The lack of emotional freedom linked to attachment may also make us feel obliged to care for the other rather than risk losing him or her. Our affection then lacks sincerity, for it's based on fear. Or we may be over-eager to help our dear one in order to ensure his or her affection. We may be over-protective, fearful something unexpected will happen to the other person, or we may be jealous when he or she has affection for others.

Love is more selfless. Instead of wondering "How can this relationship fulfill my needs?" we'll think, "What can I give to the other?" We'll accept that it's impossible for others to remove our feelings of emotional poverty and insecurity. The problem isn't that others don't satisfy our emotional needs, it's that we overemphasize our needs and expect too much.

For example, we may feel that we can't live without someone we're particularly close to. This is an exaggeration. We have our own dignity as human beings; we needn't cling to others as if they were the source of all happiness. It's helpful to remember we've lived most of our lives without being with our dear one. Furthermore, other people live very well without him or her.

This doesn't mean, however, that we should suppress our emotional needs or become aloof and independent, for that doesn't solve the problem. We must recognize our unrealistic needs and slowly seek to eliminate them. Some emotional needs may be so strong that they can't be dissolved immediately. If we try to suppress them or pretend they don't exist, we might become unduly anxious or insecure. In this case, we can try to fulfill these needs while simultaneously working gradually to subdue them.

The core problem is we seek to be loved rather than to love. We yearn to be understood by others rather than to understand them. Our sense of emotional insecurity comes from the ignorance and selfishness obscuring our minds. We can develop self-confidence by recognizing our inner potential to become a complete, satisfied and loving person. When we get in touch with our own potential to become an enlightened being with many magnificent qualities, we'll develop a true and accurate feeling of self-confidence. We'll then seek to increase our love, compassion, generosity, patience, concentration and wisdom and to share these qualities with others.

Emotional insecurity makes us continuously seek something from others. Our kindness to them is contaminated by the ulterior motive of wanting to receive something in return. However, when we recognize how much we've already received from others, we'll want to repay their kindness and our hearts will be filled with love. Love emphasizes giving rather than receiving. Not being bound by our cravings and expectations from others, we'll be open, kind and sharing, yet we'll maintain our own sense of integrity and autonomy.

Attachment wants others to be happy so much that we pressure them into doing what we think will make them happy. We give others no choice for we feel we know what's best for them. We don't allow them to do what makes them happy, nor do we accept that sometimes they'll be unhappy. Such difficulties often arise in family relationships.

Love intensely wishes others to be happy. However, it's tempered with wisdom, recognizing that whether or not others are happy also depends on them. We can guide them, but our egos won't be involved when we do. Respecting them, we'll give them the choice of whether or not to accept our advice and our help. Interestingly, when we don't pressure others to follow our advice they're more open to listening to it.

Under the influence of attachment we're bound by our emotional reactions to others. When they're nice to us we're happy. When they ignore us or speak sharply to us, we take it personally and are unhappy. But pacifying attachment doesn't mean we become hard-hearted. Rather, without attachment there will be space in our hearts for genuine affection and impartial love for others. We'll be actively involved with them.

If we subdue our attachment we can still have friends. These friendships will be richer because of the freedom and respect they'll be based on. We'll care about the happiness and misery of all beings equally, simply because everyone is the same in wanting happiness and not wanting suffering. However, our lifestyles and interests may be more compatible with those of some people. Due to close connections we've had with some people in previous lives, it will be easy to communicate with them in this lifetime. In any case, our friendships will be based on mutual interests and the wish to help each other become enlightened.

## WHEN RELATIONSHIPS END

Attachment is accompanied by the preconception that relationships last forever. Although intellectually we may know this isn't true, deep inside we long to always be with our dear ones. This clinging makes separation even more difficult, for when a dear one dies or moves away we feel as if part of ourselves were lost.

This is not to say that grief is bad. However, it's helpful to recognize that often attachment is the source of grief and depression. When our own identity is too mixed in with that of another person, we'll become depressed when we separate. When we refuse to accept deep in our hearts that life is transient, then we set ourselves up to experience pain when our dear ones die.

At the time of the Buddha, a woman was distraught when her infant died. Hysterical, she brought the dead body of her beloved child to the Buddha and asked him to revive it. The Buddha told her first to bring some mustard seeds from a home in which no one had died.

Mustard seeds were found in every home in India; however, she couldn't find a household in which no one had died. After a while she accepted in her heart that everyone dies, and the grief for her child subsided.

Bringing our understanding of impermanence from our heads to our hearts enables us also to appreciate the time we have with others. Rather than grasping for more, when more isn't available we'll rejoice at what we share with others in the present. By thus avoiding attachment, our relationships will be enriched.

# 4 *Managing Anger:*
## Transforming fear and aversion

You're working on a project, minding your own business, when a colleague comes over and tells you you're incompetent. She had entrusted you with an important job, she says, and you did it poorly. Listening to her harsh words, anger slowly yet forcefully rises in your mind and body. You lose your temper and tell her she has no right to talk to you like that. Overcome by anger, you say whatever comes into your mind, even if you know it isn't completely true. She shouts back at you, and soon everyone nearby knows what is happening.

Generally when we're angry or hurt we feel like victims of others' harmful deeds. We see ourselves as innocent people who unjustly have to bear the brunt of others' actions. We're hurt or angry because we think other people are wrong or bad. Both the anger and the hurt refuse to accept what has happened.

Many people live with a "victim mentality," constantly feeling helpless, mistreated and fearful. However, the more we understand the working of our minds and the functioning of cause and effect within our mental continuums, the more we'll understand that our present interpretations, as well as our past actions, have played vital roles in the evolution of what we experience. We are in some way responsible for what is happening to us. Knowing this, we then take responsibility and act in order to improve our situation.

To help us understand disagreeable situations and assuage our anger about them, we can ask some key questions. In examining our interpretation, we may ask, "Am I perceiving the situation accurately? Is anger an appropriate reaction?" By considering the function of cause and effect, we ask, "Why is this happening to me? Do I repeatedly find myself in similar situations? If so, why?" Let's look at these two points more in depth.

## QUESTIONING OUR INTERPRETATIONS

Are we perceiving the situation accurately? How does anger arise in us? When someone tells us our faults, it appears to us as if the pain we experience comes from the other person into us. Her words are painful in and of themselves, and we merely perceive the pain inherent in them.

If this were true, then we should be able to locate the pain in the words. She says, "You are incompetent!" Where is the unpleasant sensation? Where is the pain? Is it in "You"? In "are"? In "incompetent"? Her voice saying "You are incompetent" is sound waves. Where is the unpleasant sensation in those sound waves vibrating through the air? If you are asleep and she insults you, do you feel upset? If she says it in Mongolian (assuming you do not know that language!), do you feel hurt?

How does the pain from harsh words arise? It isn't just because our ears pick up the sound waves of a voice. We also understand their meaning. But their meaning isn't painful in and of itself, for if they were directed at someone we didn't like, the words "You are incompetent!" wouldn't be unpleasant to our ears.

The pain comes from our thinking, "She is talking to me! Me! How dare she talk to ME like this?" "I" and "me" get bigger the more we think about what happened. We look at the situation from one side—MY side—and think that's how it exists in reality. We believe our biased views are objective.

Any situation has many perspectives from which it can be viewed. When we look at a cup from above, the shape appears differently than when we look at it from the side. It would be difficult to prove that the views of our self-centered minds are the only correct ones. Thinking like this deflates our anger.

Another way to subdue our anger is to remember that something else could have happened to prompt the other person's harsh words. He may be having difficulty in another aspect of his life, and we happen to be the one he vents his anger on. It's nothing against us, so there's no reason to take it personally and be angry.

Is anger an appropriate reaction? The person who insulted us is a living being who wants to be happy and avoid any problems just as we do. The method he's using may be confused. But his wish is the same as ours: to be happy. By enlarging our perspectives and forgetting about ourselves for a minute, we'll see an unhappy human being who is angry and upset. We know what it's like to be unhappy. We know how miserable he feels right now. Why be angry at someone who is unhappy? He should be an object of our compassion.

If indeed we did make a mistake and someone points it out, why be angry? If someone tells us that we have a nose on our face, we aren't upset, because what he's saying is true. Similarly, if someone notices our mistake, what he's saying is true. The mistake is ours and we owe him an apology. He's showing us how to improve ourselves. On the other hand, if he's unjustly accusing us, why be angry? If someone says that we have horns on our head, we don't get angry because we know it's not true.

We often get angry when something we consider undesirable happens. But what use is this anger? If we can change the situation, then let's go ahead and do it. There's no need to be angry. It's very useful to think like this when confronted with social problems and injustice. They can be changed, so rather than be angry, it's wiser to work calmly to improve the society.

On the other hand, if the situation can't be changed, anger is equally useless. Once our leg is broken, we can't unbreak it. All of the corruption in the world can't be solved in a year. Getting angry at something we can't alter makes us miserable. Worrying about or fearing something that hasn't happened immobilizes us. Shantideva said in *A Guide to the Bodhisattva's Way of Life*:

> Why be unhappy about something
> If it can be remedied?
> And what is the use of being unhappy about something
> If it cannot be remedied?

## CONSIDERING CAUSE AND EFFECT

The working of cause and effect is a central idea in Buddhism. This will be explained more fully in a later chapter; however, the principal meaning is that our actions bring results. All the results of an action aren't immediately known to us, for just as it takes time for a seed to sprout and become a tree, so too is time needed for our actions to bear their results.

As we come to understand the functioning of cause and effect, we'll understand that the situations we encounter in life don't happen to us by accident. They result from actions we have done in the past. Just as a boomerang circles around and returns to whoever threw it, so too are we treated the way we've treated others. The Buddhist explanation of cause and effect is similar to the Christian idea "As thou sow, so shall thou reap."

If we examine how we've acted towards others, we'll see that our own attitudes and behavior haven't always been exemplary. We've broken up friendships, insulted, abused and gossiped about others and taken their belongings. Is it any wonder we receive harm ourselves? Maybe we didn't recently mistreat the particular person who harms us right now, but we have harmed others in the past. When the fruits of our own actions ripen, there's no benefit in becoming angry or wallowing in self-pity, for ultimately our own energy put us in that situation. As the great Indian sage Shantideva said:

Why did I previously commit those actions
Because of which others now cause me harm?
Since everything is related to my actions
Why should I bear malice towards those (who harm
   me now)?

This isn't suggesting that we become masochistic and aggressively blame ourselves. Rather, we'll recognize our role and will learn from it. If we don't like the results we're experiencing now, we'll make a strong determination to stop creating causes for similar things to occur in the future. This will make us mindful not to harm others. The next time we're about to lose our temper, we'll think twice. Learning from the situation, we'll make a strong decision to improve ourselves. By doing this, we'll transform a disturbing situation into a beneficial one.

Do we often find ourselves in similar situations, repeatedly reacting in similar ways? If so, why? We can examine to see if we're habitually careless, obliging others to correct our mistakes. If this is the case, the other person is in fact kind to point out our mistake, for it gives us the opportunity to improve. The fact that he may be doing so in a loud voice isn't relevant. The point is we need to be more aware of how our actions affect others. This person is helping us to develop such awareness.

We can also observe whether we habitually feel hurt or angry when we face criticism. Sometimes we're too sensitive and easily offended. If someone acts in a way we don't particularly like, we exaggerate its importance, making it concrete and unforgettable. Then we carry a grudge with us for years. This is the root of many a family feud.

Our holding a grudge doesn't hurt the other person, for she may have forgotten about the incident long ago. But our grudge makes us miserable for years. The other person said the words once, but we say them over and over for years, causing ourselves pain each time. For our own benefit, as well as for harmony with others, it's advantageous to be less sensitive and to let things go.

## PUSHY OR PASSIVE?

Does that mean we let people push us around? Do we let someone harm himself or others because stopping him would involve raising our voice or striking him? No. Being patient doesn't mean being placid. A patient person is one whose mind is serene. The actions following from a patient mind may be forceful or mild.

First we must free our mind from anger. When we notice we're regarding the situation through the narrow outlook of ME, we'll stop and spend some time enlarging our perspective. We'll think about how the situation appears to the other person and what is important to him. We'll reflect on how our own actions in the past and present drew us into the situation.

Once our anger is stilled, there will be space for compassion and patience. A clear mind, free from short-sighted and turbulent anger, can realistically examine alternative ways to act and decide which is best for everyone concerned.

To communicate effectively we sometimes need to speak forcefully. Speaking strongly but with a compassionate attitude in a situation that calls for it is an important skill. It's quite different than shouting with uncontrolled anger when it would have been more skillful to be silent, to apologize or to respectfully explain our side. The motivation, which is our internal state of mind, isn't to be confused with the verbal and physical actions we use to communicate to others.

Whenever possible we should avoid violent actions. If, to stop someone from harming himself or others, the only solution is to strike him, then, with compassion for the harmed and the harmer, we should do only what is required to stop him. Thus, it's important to have a peaceful mind before acting. If we act under the influence of anger, we're likely to use physical or verbal force when it's not necessary, or when it is, to use more than is required.

In order to communicate we may sometimes have to speak firmly—to state our understanding of what is correct and incorrect, beneficial or not beneficial. This can be done without anger. But if the other person speaks falsely or angrily and we do too, who is right and who is wrong? Anger corrupts what we say and do. A calm mind can deal with the situation in a beneficial way.

# 5 Closed-Mindedness:
## Dealing with differences

Closed-mindedness is an attitude that doesn't want to look at a new idea or event. It makes us tight, prejudiced and defensive. It arises, for example, when certain controversial subjects come up at the dinner table. With closed-mindedness we react like an ostrich: we want to "stick our heads in the ground" and not examine any new idea which could shake our stubborn conceptions.

Such an attitude brings many problems in our lives. If we examine history, we can see how detrimental closed-mindedness has been to human development. Closed-mindedness made people oppose scientific investigation in the Middle Ages; closed-minded fear made people in Europe ignore the murder of millions of innocent people under the Nazi regime. Closed-mindedness also condones racial, religious and gender prejudice.

Looking beneath the closed-minded attitude, we find a preconceived idea that we have everything figured out and we don't want to be shaken by new ideas. We have a subtle fear that should the sandcastle of our world-view be shattered by a new idea, we would be lost. Consequently, we would rather be stubborn and not listen, or forget about it and watch television, go gambling, or get drunk. It's clear how closed-mindedness makes us tight and uncomfortable.

Seeing the pitfalls of closed-mindedness, we'll endeavor to develop an intelligent approach to new ideas and events. We'll listen to new ideas and examine them with logic in an intelligent, unbiased way. With the intention of improving our understanding and contributing to world peace and human development, we'll listen to new ideas and proposals. Whether or not we later accept an idea, we'll learn something by examining it intelligently, and our understanding will become clearer.

Being open-minded, however, doesn't mean we accept every new idea we run across. This is especially true in the "spiritual supermarket" existing in the West now. Nor does open-mindedness mean we so desperately want to be modern that we throw out our rich cultural heritage and blindly follow every new idea or scheme.

With open minds, we'll be tolerant. Having logically examined a new idea and checked for evidence to validate it, if we decide we don't agree with it, we can still be calm and friendly with another person who does. Disagreeing with an idea doesn't mean that we hate a person who accepts it. The idea and the person are different. Also, people's ideas change. We can appreciate what others say—be it correct or nonsensical—because it challenges us to think and thus to increase our wisdom.

When we find ourselves across the table from a person talking about a new subject or idea, we can approach the conversation with joy in learning, rather than with a judgmental attitude that has already decided the other person is wrong. We'll let ourselves listen, reflect, grow and share, while we re-examine our previous ideas.

Such an approach is beneficial in many circumstances. For example, we'll encourage our colleagues, boss and subordinates to give feedback about past projects and to suggest future improvements. Such openness improves the atmosphere at work. With open minds, we can then accurately evaluate their ideas and can work together with others for our mutual benefit. Although a boss will still have authority, he or she no longer will be authoritarian.

We don't have to defend our ideas or beliefs. There's nothing in an idea that makes it inherently ours. If someone criticizes our ideas, it doesn't mean that we're stupid. Also, there's no need to fear losing face should we re-evaluate an idea and change our minds. Fear of seeming foolish if our ideas are proved incorrect comes from caring more about having a good reputation than about discerning what is true. With open minds, we'll approach every idea and situation as an opportunity to learn and to share with others.

# 6  *Accurately Viewing Ourselves:*
Antidotes for false pride

Pride is a conception, a way of viewing things, in which we inflate a quality we possess—physical beauty or strength, education, social class or talent—and consider ourselves far superior to others.

Such an attitude has many disadvantages. Under the influence of pride, we make sure that others know how good we are. We talk about our achievements; we seek to impress others in order to gain praise, reputation and money. Pride makes us look down upon others who we think lack our good qualities.

When overcome by self-importance, we're actually rather pathetic. If we were honest with ourselves, we would see that under the masquerade we don't really believe we're good. To convince ourselves otherwise, we desperately try to persuade others that we have a certain excellent quality. We think that if others believe we're great, then we must be. Deep inside, all of us ordinary beings have poor images of ourselves. Even the person with a dignified appearance who seems to be the epitome of success according to worldly standards doesn't feel good enough. Finding it difficult to admit our insecurity to ourselves, we mask it by being proud.

How is it possible that people who appear to be successful

don't feel good about themselves? They, like us, look to external sources for self-validation, praise and acceptance. Thus, we're unaware of our potentials to become completely wise and compassionate. Although we look outside for happiness and self-respect, these qualities can only be truly attained by internal development.

Pride makes us act in ridiculous ways: we show off our physical appearance, often appearing silly in the eyes of others. We freely criticize others and then are puzzled when people don't like to be in our company. We treat others unjustly and then complain there's no harmony in the society. Disharmony occurs in any group when people are proud and neglect others' feelings.

Although proud people demand that others respect them, respect can't be forced. In fact, society respects those who are humble. None of the recipients of the Nobel Peace Prize is boisterous and arrogant. When His Holiness the Dalai Lama received this great award in 1989, he attributed it not to himself, but to the sincere altruistic attitude and the actions flowing from compassion.

We can respect everyone. People who are poorer, less educated or talented than we are have many qualities and abilities that we lack. Every being deserves respect simply because he or she has feelings. Everyone deserves to be at least listened to. Proud people can't appreciate this and are condescending and intolerant. Confident people are kind, humble and learn from everyone. In this way, they generate harmony and mutual respect among others.

Pride is one of the chief obstacles to increasing wisdom and developing inner potential. Believing themselves to be learned, talented and excellent, proud people are self-complacent. They don't want to and cannot learn from others. Their pride imprisons them in a stagnant state.

## SELF-CONFIDENCE

Often pride is confused with self-confidence, and humility is mistaken for a poor self-concept. However, acting arrogantly doesn't mean we're self-confident, and being humble doesn't mean that we have a poor self-image. People who are self-confident are also humble, for they have nothing to defend or to prove to the world.

It's very difficult to look at ourselves objectively. We tend to under- or overestimate ourselves, swinging between the extremes of thinking we're useless and unlovable to believing we're fantastic. Neither view is an accurate evaluation of ourselves, for we all have some good qualities as well as some traits that need to be improved.

We can't eliminate our faults by concealing them or by arrogantly competing with others to prove we're best. But we can honestly acknowledge our weaknesses and try to correct them. Similarly, self-confidence comes not from conceitedly proclaiming our qualities, but from examining our talents and abilities to develop them.

In this line, it's helpful to remember that we have the potential to become a Buddha, one who has eliminated all obscurations and fully developed all beneficial qualities. This may initially sound like an extravagant assertion, but as we begin to understand Buddha nature and the path to enlightenment, our conviction in its validity will increase. The chapter "Buddha Nature," and the section "The Path to Enlightenment" will make this clearer. This precious Buddha nature is our birthright. It can never be lost or taken from us. Knowing this, we'll have a stable and realistic basis for self-confidence.

We can accept ourselves for what we are and have faith in our ability to become kinder and wiser people. This balanced view of ourselves also gives us mental space to appreciate and respect others, for all beings have some qualities worthy of respect. Self-confident people are able to admit what they don't know, and are consequently happy and willing to learn from others. In this way, their own good qualities and knowledge increase.

When we possess good qualities, others will naturally perceive them. There's no need for us to proclaim them. Mahatma

Gandhi is a good example of this. Living and dressing simply, he avoided praising himself and instead respected others. Although he avoided broadcasting his virtues, his successful work and greatness as a human being were evident to others.

## PACIFYING PRIDE

What techniques can we employ to counteract pride? Since pride is a mistaken and narrow attitude, developing a broad view enables us to see the situation more realistically. In this way, we can reduce our pride.

If we are proud because of our education, for example, we need only realize all our knowledge is due to the kind efforts of our teachers. When we were born, we were very ignorant and incapable: we couldn't even feed ourselves or say what we needed. Everything we know—even how to speak or how to tie our shoes—comes from the kindness of others who have taught us. What, then, is there to be proud of? Without others' care and attention, we would know very little and would have few skills. Thinking like this frees us from pride.

Likewise, if we're proud because we have money, we can remember the money hasn't always been ours. If it came from our family or from an inheritance, gratitude to those people is more appropriate than pride in ourselves. Even if we earned the money, it still came from others—from our employers, employees and clients. Due to the employer who gave us the job, or our employees who helped the business prosper, we now have money. In this sense, these people have been very kind to us.

We may not be used to remembering the kindness of others in this way, but if we think about it, we'll see it's reasonable. Although we may feel that we succeed despite the ill will of others, in fact our own effort alone isn't sufficient to bring success. We're dependent on others. Knowing this, wise people feel gratitude—not pride—towards others.

We may be proud of our youth, beauty, strength or prowess, but these are changing qualities. We may feel that we'll be young, beautiful, strong or athletic for a long time, but these are fleeting attributes. Moment by moment we're aging. The wrinkles don't come suddenly, the teeth don't fall out at once; but gradually, our bodies lose their luster.

Our society tries to prevent aging or cover it up, but in fact the muscular football player is on his way to becoming an old man who will sit by the sidelines holding a cane. The beauty queen inevitably will become a bent-over old lady. Seeing that our bodies are constantly aging, what is there now to be proud of?

If our bodies are able and attractive, we can appreciate those qualities without being conceited. Similarly, we can rejoice at whatever talents, good fortune or knowledge we have, but not be haughty and smug. Instead, we'll use whatever qualities we have to benefit others.

To subdue pride regarding our intelligence, we can contemplate a difficult subject. Doing this makes us recognize our limitations and automatically dispels pride. With a more balanced view of ourselves, we'll use our energy to improve ourselves and to help others.

# 7  *From Jealousy To Joy:*
## Letting go of a painful heart

When we're jealous, we can't bear the happiness, wealth, reputation, talents and good qualities of others. We want to destroy their happiness and good qualities, and claim them for ourselves. We may mask our jealousy or rationalize it, but when we strip away these shields, we starkly see how ugly it is.

Jealousy can fester in relationships. We're jealous of another person because he or she is with our dear one. It arises in work situations when someone else receives the job we want. When another person can play soccer better than we can, is a better guitarist, has more stylish clothes or was admitted to a better school, we get jealous. Jealousy is involved in many border disputes between nations and in disharmony among political parties within a nation.

Sometimes our jealousy is so intense that we can't sleep at night or concentrate on our work. Jealousy leads us to say or do things which destroy others' well-being and happiness. It makes us manipulative and dishonest.

Jealousy is based on our incorrect interpretation of a situation. Extremely self-centered, jealousy thinks, "My happiness is more important that any one else's. I can't endure another person having the happiness that I want."

The antidote is to look at the situation with a more open mind, considering not only our own happiness, profit and loss, but also that of others. There can be a profound effect on our minds when we remember that others want happiness: they're glad to receive possessions and good opportunities, they enjoy the company of nice people, and they appreciate praise.

When someone else receives something good, why not rejoice? We often say how wonderful it would be if others were happy. Now one person is happy and we didn't even have to do anything to bring it about! There is no purpose in making ourselves miserable by being jealous.

We don't always have to be the best or have the best. A small child cries, argues and tries to ruin his playmate's fun when the playmate gets something he doesn't. As adults responsible for setting a good example for children, and as citizens responsible for harmony in society, it's beneficial if we allow ourselves to be happy and rejoice at others' good fortune. In that way, both we and the other person will be happy.

For example, a colleague receives the promotion we thought we deserved. If we look at it only from our own viewpoint, we're miserable and jealous. Jealousy makes neither the other person nor ourselves happy. It also accomplishes nothing, for our jealousy doesn't deprive her of the promotion and grant it to us instead. If we remember that the other person is happy about the promotion and would like others to join in her happiness, we'll rejoice at her good fortune. Then both of us will be happy.

It's easier to correct our unrealistic attitude of jealousy when it concerns something small: for example someone receives a gift and we don't. It's more difficult to rejoice in others' happiness when it means a loss on our own part.

Take, for example, a couple relationship in which one partner is unfaithful. If we react with jealousy and then shout, curse and even beat the other, we don't alleviate the pain of our jealousy, nor do we convince the other person that it's good to stay with us. Allowing the fire of jealousy to continue burning, we're restless, miserable and vengeful. In addition, we're likely to say or do something that will make the other person dislike us, thus preventing reconciliation.

Although we don't condone the other person's improper behavior, if we can remain calm, we won't experience as much pain. Also, we'll be able to keep communication open between us. In this way, both of us will feel comfortable when we meet or talk together later. The door will remain open should the other wish to apologize.

In short, freeing ourselves from jealousy eliminates our own internal torture. Rejoicing at others' good qualities and success brings happiness to both ourselves and others.

# 8  *Catching the Thief:*
## Recognizing the disturbing attitudes

In order to recognize the disturbing attitudes when they deviously appear in our minds, we need mindfulness and introspective alertness. Once we've made the determination to act, speak and think in beneficial ways, mindfulness prevents us from getting distracted. Introspective alertness makes us aware of what we are doing, saying and thinking, and if it notices a disturbing attitude, it alerts us to the danger. The Kadampa Buddhist tradition in Tibet recommends:

> When sitting alone, watch your mind.
> When in public, watch your speech.

Because our lives are busy, we're often unaware of what is going on inside us. We're preoccupied with going here and there, doing this and planning that. After a while we feel we don't know ourselves very well, since our attention is always directed outwards. To remedy this, it's important to have some "quiet time" each day, time to relax and be alone. We can read some helpful literature, or just sit and reflect. It's good to review what has happened each day: what we did and why, what others said and did and how we reacted, what we thought and felt that was expressed and unexpressed.

This quiet time gives us the opportunity to "digest" what we experience, to be aware of what we thought and felt. We may observe that we were sympathetic to someone's difficulty; we may discover that we didn't get upset in a situation that would generally have disturbed us. We'll see progress in our cultivation of positive mindstates and will rejoice and congratulate ourselves—without getting proud of course!

On the other hand, we may notice an uncomfortable feeling and ask ourselves, "Was I angry then? Was I jealous? Attached? Proud? Closed-minded?" Being honest with ourselves, we'll be willing to admit when we had unrealistic or harmful attitudes. There's no need to judge ourselves for having them. They are simply there. We're ordinary beings, so naturally destructive emotions sometimes arise. There's no reason to feel guilty about them, nor should we ignore them.

To resolve these uncomfortable emotions, we can practice the techniques explained in the preceding chapters. For example, we may notice that our interpretation of a situation was narrow, causing us to become angry. If we examine closely, we can pinpoint the falsity of that projection. We'll then try to see the situation from a more realistic and kind viewpoint. In this way, we'll let go of the uncomfortable emotion. Afterwards, we can determine to be more mindful in the future, so that we won't physically and verbally act upon such disturbing attitudes.

Over a period of time, we'll notice that one of the disturbing attitudes occurs more frequently in us than the others. This is the one to be especially aware of in our daily lives. During our quiet time each day, we can gradually train ourselves in a more open and compassionate perspective. Thus, our beneficial outlooks will become more habitual, and situations will begin to appear differently to us. Then, when similar events arise during the day, we'll have a better chance of catching the false projections and disturbing attitudes before they take charge of us.

By gradually freeing ourselves from wrong conceptions and transforming our mental outlook, we'll enjoy life much more and will be of more benefit to others. In this way, our lives can become very meaningful.

# 9 *The Culprit:*
## Selfishness

Our personality comprises many different factors, some of them contradictory to each other. Sometimes we're loving and other times we're spiteful. At times we're proud and reject advice; other times we're inquisitive and eager to learn. We don't have a fixed personality since our characteristics can change. By becoming more habituated to constructive attitudes and less accustomed to the harmful ones, our character can improve.

The disturbing attitudes aren't an intrinsic part of us. They're like clouds covering the vastness and clarity of the sky, and therefore they can change and vanish. Because they're based on misinterpretations and projections, the disturbing attitudes can't be sustained once we realize their falsity. Thus, as our wisdom and compassion increase, the disturbing attitudes diminish.

This doesn't happen just by our wishing for it or praying for it. It happens when we've created the causes for it to occur. As we gradually subdue the disturbing attitudes in our daily life, a resultant peaceful state of mind naturally emerges. We're responsible. We have control. The clear nature of our mind is always there, waiting to be revealed when the clouds of the disturbing attitudes are dispelled. This is our human beauty; this is our potential.

The Buddha said that our disturbing attitudes share two common factors: ignorance and selfishness. We don't understand who we are or how we and other phenomena exist. This is ignorance. Out of ignorance, we put a disproportionate emphasis on me, I, my and mine. This self-cherishing attitude then proceeds to bring us many problems, even though it seemingly protects our well-being.

The philosophy of the self-cherishing mind is, "I'm the most important. My happiness is the most crucial, and my misery should be eliminated first." This seems like a rather childish attitude, but when we check our own thoughts we may find that many of our actions are motivated by the attitude of "my happiness now is the most important."

This is a habitual attitude we've had since birth (maybe even before!). Although babies don't think in words, they cry for food not only because their stomachs are empty, but also because their minds are craving for "my happiness now." Our society nurtures the selfish mind, teaching us to seek our own happiness at almost any cost. Although competition needn't be selfish, it most often is, for how often do we rejoice when the other person or team is better than we are?

We're taught to manipulate and cheat in order to get what we want, and as long as our dishonesty isn't discovered it's secretly condoned. The large number of government officials and corporate executives facing prosecution illustrates this. However, rather than gleefully pointing the finger at them, we must look within ourselves to see if we act similarly.

As adults, we're more deceptive than children, for we mask our selfish attitudes in polite manners and apparent consideration for others. But underneath, we value ourselves the most and others come second.

Some people believe that human beings are selfish by nature, that we and our selfishness are as inseparable as perfume and its scent. It seems this way because our selfish viewpoint has existed for a long time. In that sense, we may say it's natural, because as babies we were self-centered and we'll continue to be so until we make an effort to change.

However, this doesn't mean selfishness is an inseparable part of us. If it were, how could some of the great religious leaders have cherished others more than themselves? How could a mother cherish her child more than herself? Why would people risk their lives to save others?

If we were inherently selfish, there would be no way to train ourselves in impartial love and compassion for all. However, such a method exists. Many people throughout the ages have succeeded in transforming their attitudes and actually cherish others more than themselves.

If selfishness were an intrinsic part of us, it also would mean the view of the selfish mind would be an accurate and beneficial way to relate to the world. But as we'll see, it isn't.

Selfishness can be decreased and finally removed from our mindstreams. First, we must recognize the disadvantages of the self-cherishing attitude. Being convinced that it's the cause of all unsought problems, we'll then investigate how it operates and eliminate it.

The self-cherishing thought seems to be our friend, looking out for our welfare, protecting us from harms and ensuring our happiness. But does it? Whenever there is conflict between two people, two groups or two countries, selfishness is present. One side is protecting its interests, thinking they're the most critical, and the other is doing the same. Compromise and cooperation become difficult, as does forgiveness.

For example, in a family conflict, if we don't get our way we're unhappy. If we win we may temporarily be "happy," but deep inside we aren't pleased about what we said or did in order to get our way. Unbridled selfishness doesn't make us a better and more respectable person, even though it may give us temporary power. When we cherish ourselves foremost, how can others completely trust us?

Another disadvantage of the selfish mind is that it makes our problems appear to be greater than they are. We have a small difficulty, but by contemplating it repeatedly, the problem grows and grows until we can think of nothing else. "My exam is so crucial!'' ''My boss is demanding too much!'' Our preoccupation with small problems makes them take on enormous proportions with earth-shattering consequences. We complain, we can't sleep, we may start drinking and taking drugs or even have a nervous breakdown. In short, the self-cherishing attitude is a magnet attracting problems to ourselves.

## THE "LOGIC" OF THE SELFISH ATTITUDE

The primary tenet of the selfish mind is that we are the center of the universe, the most important one, whose happiness and miseries are the most crucial. Why do I feel I'm the most important? "Because I'm me," says the selfish attitude, "I'm not you."

I feel I'm the center of the universe (although I'm much too discreet to say that publicly). But so do you, and so do many other people. Just feeling that our happiness is the most important doesn't make it so.

What proof do we have that our happiness is the most important? Does my toothache hurt more than yours? Is my pleasure from eating greater than that of a beggar? When we examine it logically, can any of us say that the happiness or sorrow we experience is any more intense or important than others'?

We may feel that because we are the head of a family, the director of a company or a skilled and talented person we're more important than others. Yes, we are, but only because we have more responsibility to serve and help others because of our position. However, that doesn't mean that our happiness feels better and our pain worse than those of others. The Indian sage Shantideva says in *A Guide to the Bodhisattva's Way of Life*:

> When both myself and others
> Are similar in that we wish to be happy,
> What is so special about me?
> Why do I strive for my happiness alone?

The rich and the poor, the intelligent and the average, the

beautiful and the ugly all want to be happy and avoid any misery. We may have different ways in which we find happiness, but the fact of wanting happiness is common to us all. In this way, every being is equal. As Shantideva says:

> Hence I should dispel the misery of others
> Because it is suffering, just like my own,
> And I should benefit others
> Because they are beings, just like myself.

It's important to recognize that although all of us want happiness, we all have different ways of getting it. We like different things and have different cultural values and individual goals. It would be self-centered to think that because we value something, everyone else must also. Many misunderstandings arise cross-culturally and between generations because we assume that other people should value what we do. It's extremely important to be aware of and respect others' likes and dislikes, whether they're the same as ours or not.

This is a call to look beyond superficial similarities among people and focus on the deeper level. Superficially, we may think, "You're interested in chemistry. I find that boring, but ancient history is interesting," or "You want your country to be more modern and I wish my country would slow down and get more in touch with nature."

If we concentrate on these differences, we feel isolated from others. However, if we look deeper and see that on a very basic level we're the same in wanting happiness and not wanting suffering, we'll feel very close to others. Feeling we have something in common with everyone, we'll then be able to communicate better with others. Shantideva queries:

> In the same way as the hands and so forth
> Are regarded as limbs of the body,
> Likewise why are embodied beings
> Not regarded as limbs of life?

When we step on a thorn, our hand reaches down and pulls the thorn from our foot. The hand doesn't hesitate. It doesn't think, "Why doesn't the foot take care of itself? It's so inconvenient for me to help it." Why does the hand help the foot so easily? Because they're seen as part of the same unit, our body.

Similarly, if we regard all beings as part of a unit—life—then we won't feel disturbed by helping others. We'll be aiding another part of the larger unit of which we're a part. Instead of conceiving of ourselves as independent people, we'll understand that in fact we're interdependent. Thus, we'll help others as if we were helping ourselves.

In this way, we'll render aid free of pride. When the hand helps the foot, it doesn't think, "I'm so great! Look at me. I sacrifice so much for this foot. I hope the foot appreciates what I'm doing for it!" The hand just helps. There's no condescension or pride.

Likewise, there's no reason for us to boast of how much we do for others. If we habituate ourselves to the idea that we're all part of one unit of life, helping others will be as simple as helping ourselves is now.

By repeatedly contemplating the equality of ourselves and others, we can eliminate selfishness from our mindstreams. When a light is turned on in a room, the darkness automatically vanishes. Similarly, when the false interpretations and preconceptions of our self-centered approach are exposed by deep understanding, the selfish attitude vanishes. By repeatedly familiarizing ourselves with an altruistic attitude, it will become as natural as selfishness is now.

Self-cherishing is a state of mind that is reflected in our actions. However, we can't evaluate others' degree of selfishness and altruism merely by their actions. For example, one person may flamboyantly give a thousand dollars to charity with the motivation to appear generous to her friends. Another person may humbly contribute five dollars to a charity with the sincere wish that others receive benefit. In fact, the latter person is the generous one, while the former is stingily seeking a good reputation.

RESOLVING DOUBTS

Some people may feel guilty that they're selfish. This is completely unproductive. Self-reproach is a clever trick of the selfish mind, for it again puts the emphasis on "me" and "how bad I am."

What is needed isn't guilt but action. When we notice that we're being selfish, we can remember that others want happiness as much as we do. We can try to feel how happy they would be if we helped them. Remembering the kindness all beings showed us in past and present lives, we'll want to return their care. In this way, our selfish attitude will automatically diminish, while the wish to help others will increase.

Eliminating our selfishness doesn't mean we give everyone everything they want. Altruism must be coupled with wisdom. To give an alcoholic a drink isn't compassion. To allow a child to grow up without discipline isn't benefiting him or her.

Nor does subduing self-cherishing entail always giving in to others and never defending our own views. When there's a difference of opinion between ourselves and others, it's wise first to free our minds from anger and attachment. If we stubbornly cling to our own view simply because it's ours, we're limiting ourselves. If we close-mindedly refuse to try out another's idea, we can't learn. But, when we clear our minds of all disturbing attitudes, we can look at the situation with a spacious perspective and seek the best solution for the most people. We still may favor our previous proposal, but our minds will be calm. Or, we may change our opinion.

Some people assert, "If we weren't selfish, we wouldn't have any ambition in life and would be passive and without goals." Although selfish motives may now drive our attempts to get good results on our exams, win a high position in a company or invent new devices, it doesn't mean that we must necessarily abandon those activities if we free ourselves from the bonds of the self-cherishing thought.

Of course, we'll give up some activities when we stop seeking our own benefit. For example, we'll refrain from abusing and criticizing others. But other actions can still be pursued with another, more compassionate motivation. We can strive to do well in school in order to gain knowledge that can be used to benefit others. We can invent things or do business with the attitude of using our skills to serve others. We can abandon competition done with a self-centered attitude and replace it with doing our best in order to benefit others.

Although other people in the business world may continue to work with a selfish motivation, that doesn't prevent us from changing ours. One Hong Kong executive told me from her experience that when we conduct business ethically and have genuine concern for our clients, suppliers and so on, they trust us. By having a good relationship with them, they continue to do business with us and refer others to us as well. If we are selfishly concerned with getting the most money and best deal for ourselves, it won't be profitable in the long run. Her conclusion was that good ethics and concern for others improve business!

Diminishing our selfishness doesn't mean we stop having the will to live or no longer defend ourselves when in danger. Killing others isn't the only possible way of responding to danger. We're humans and can use our intelligence and creativity to solve problems without resorting to violence.

With compassion for the person who is harming us, we can stop him because we don't want him to reap the ill effects of his action and because we would like to prolong our life in order to serve others more. Although we may never have thought in this way before, it's not an impractical or impossible way to think. By training our mind in the kind heart, it will grow within us.

## THE NECESSITY OF A KIND HEART

A kind heart is the essential cause of happiness. Being kind to others is the nicest thing we can do for ourselves. When we respect others and are considerate of their needs, opinions and wishes, hostility evaporates. It takes two people to fight, and if we refuse to be one of them, there is no quarrel.

Our loving-kindness can manifest in small deeds. For example, with consideration for our common environment, we'll recycle our newspaper, glass and cans. When someone is in a hurry, we'll let her go ahead of us in line. We won't complain when our tax money is used to educate and find jobs for the poor.

In the long run, the more we help others, the happier we'll be. We live in a world in which we're dependent on each other, so the more others are happy, the more pleasant our environment will be. As His Holiness the Dalai Lama says, "If you want to be selfish, then be wisely selfish. The best way to do that is to help others."

When people are agitated, it's often best not to respond immediately, but to wait until they have calmed down before discussing the problem. In that way, there's no danger that we'll react to their anger with our own. In addition, when people are upset they generally aren't able to listen and discuss, while if we let them settle down and approach them later, it's often more fruitful.

Of course, each situation is different. If someone wants to talk about a problem and we condescendingly say, "Oh, you're irrational now. I'm not going to talk to you," it doesn't help! A kind heart isn't condescending, it's skillful and caring.

I asked the participants in a workshop to role-play a conflict situation from their lives. The first time, they played the scene with two angry, stubborn people, each viewing the situation from their own self-centered perspective. The second time, they played it with one person being argumentative and the other listening and understanding his position. We were astounded at how different the two versions of the same event were!

With a kind heart we'll be harmonious with people of other religious beliefs, for there's nothing to be gained by quarreling with people of other religions. At work or with our family, there will be the possibility of resolving differences of opinion. People in the fields of communication and conflict resolution recognize the value of a kind heart to bring agreement. Therapists and family counselors emphasize the need for a kind heart to ease a person's internal and external conflict.

A kind heart is the root of harmony and mutual respect. It prevents us from feeling estranged or fearful of others. It also protects us from becoming angry, attached, closed-minded, proud or jealous. When opportunities arise to help others we won't lack courage or compassion. If political leaders had impartial minds and kind hearts, how different our world would be!

As all problems arise from the self-cherishing attitude, it would be wise for each of us, as individuals, to exert ourselves to subdue it. World peace doesn't come from winning a war, nor can it be legislated. Peace comes through each person eliminating his or her own selfishness and developing a kind heart. This will certainly not come about tomorrow; however, we can each do our part beginning today. The beneficial result in our own lives will immediately be evident.

# PART III

# OUR CURRENT SITUATION

# 1 *Rebirth:*
## Bridging life to life

In many countries and in many cultures people believe in rebirth: that our present life is one in a series of lives. Although our present existence seems so real and so sure, it doesn't last forever. Our lives come to an end. Death, however, doesn't signify the end of our existence. It marks a transition in which our minds leave our present bodies and are reborn in others.

Some things, such as flowers and mountains, can be known directly through our senses: we see, hear, smell, taste and touch them. To know other things, we use logic. For example, we can't see the fire in a distant place, but we infer its existence because we see the smoke. To know many things, we depend on the testimony of reliable people. For example, we ourselves haven't done certain scientific experiments, but we accept the conclusions of reliable scientists who have.

The upcoming subjects—rebirth, karma and cyclic existence—can't be known through our senses. We can't see someone's mind leaving one body and entering another. Nor can we see all of the long-term ramifications of a particular action. Our eyes can't detect all the various life forms in the universe. These subjects must be examined by logic and by hearing the experiences of reliable people. Then we can make our own decision about whether or not they exist.

It takes time to investigate and think about rebirth, cause and effect, and cyclic existence. When we approach these subjects, it's advisable to temporarily set aside whatever preconceptions we may have about how and why we came into existence. Listen, read and reflect with an open mind. Discuss these topics with others in a spirit of free inquiry that seeks to know the truth. Experiment with the theories of rebirth and karma: provisionally accept them and then see if they can explain things that previously you had no explanation for.

## PEOPLE WHO REMEMBER

Although most of us are unable to remember our previous lives, some people have that ability. To hear about their experiences can help us to understand rebirth.

The Tibetans have a system of searching for, testing, and identifying the reincarnations of realized spiritual masters. I'd like to share with you the stories of how two Tibetan spiritual masters I know personally were identified.

Just after the Thirteenth Dalai Lama, the religious and political leader of Tibet, passed away in 1933, signs indicating the whereabouts of his future incarnation appeared: the head of his lifeless body turned to face northeast, a rare fungus grew on the northeast pillar in the room where his tomb was, and rainbows and auspicious cloud formations appeared on the northeast sky of Tibet's capital, Lhasa.

The spiritual master who was then the regent of Tibet went to Lhamo Latso, a lake high in the mountains where people often see visions. On the surface of the lake he saw the appearance of the three Tibetan letters *A*, *KA* and *MA* and a landscape. The landscape contained a three-storied monastery with a gold and jade roof on a hill and a road leading to a house with a turquoise-colored tile fringe around the roof. A brown and white dog stood in the courtyard.

Later a search party disguised as merchants on a trading excursion was sent to Amdo in northeastern Tibet. In Tibet travelers often seek food and shelter from the local farmers, and as the party approached a certain farmhouse, a brown dog in the courtyard barked at them. They noticed that the house matched the description of the one the regent saw in the lake, and the location of the village corresponded to the letters which appeared in the lake: it was in Amdo, near Kumbum, and the local monastery was called Karma (*KA* and *MA*) Shartsong Hermitage.

When the leader of the party, disguised as a servant, went into the kitchen, a young boy climbed on his lap. The child started to play with the rosary around the leader's neck and told him he was a teacher from Sera Monastery. The young boy also identified the government official posing as the head merchant and spoke to them in the Lhasa dialect, known by the previous Dalai Lama but not by the young child's current family or the people of Amdo. Later he correctly identified a walking stick, ritual implements and the glasses of the previous Dalai Lama, which had been placed among others that were similar to them. In this way, the child came to be recognized as the Fourteenth Dalai Lama, who is the religious and political leader of Tibetans today.

Zopa Rinpoche's story is also extraordinary. For over twenty years, in a cave in a remote area in Solokumbu, Nepal, the Lawudo Lama Kunzang Yeshe diligently pursued his spiritual practice in solitary retreat. The neighboring villagers asked him to help with the education of their children, and he promised that in the future he would build a school for the young monks of the area. However, he continued his solitary practice and passed away in meditation around 1945.

In 1946 a child was born in Thami, a village across the steep river gorge from Lawudo. When the child could barely toddle, he would repeatedly set off in the direction of Lawudo. His sister would have to run after him and bring him home before he got too far or hurt himself on the mountain paths. When he was old enough to speak, he told them, "I am the Lawudo Lama and I want to go to my cave."

Later, he was recognized as the incarnation of the Lawudo

Lama and named Zopa Rinpoche. One of his first deeds as an adult was to set up a monastery school in the Kathmandu Valley principally for the young monks of the Solokumbu area. Despite his busy life with many disciples and frequent trips to Western countries to teach, Zopa Rinpoche still gives the impression of a mountain meditator. "He carries his cave with him as he travels," we joke, for he sleeps only one hour a night, sitting up at that, and he easily goes in and out of meditation as we talk with him.

Remembering previous lives is not confined to realized spiritual masters. Many ordinary children do as well. Francis Story did extensive research on such cases, and wrote of them in his book *Rebirth as Doctrine and Experience.* For example, in 1964, Sunil Dutt of Bareilly, India, at the age of four told his parents that he was Seth Krishna, the owner of a school in Budaun, India. His parents took him there, and he at once recognized the building and knew his way around. He went to the principal's office and was dismayed to see a stranger there. In fact, the principal Seth Krishna had appointed had been changed. The boy remarked that the sign bearing his name on the facade of the building was no longer there and indicated where it had formerly been.

On going to the Shri Krishna Oil Mill, Sunil called for an old servant by name, recognized Seth Krishna's elder sister and brother-in-law, and also identified Seth Krishna in a group photograph. His meeting with Seth Krishna's widow was especially poignant. He asked her about a particular religious object belonging to the family and recognized his previous wardrobe. Many other cases of previous life recall were investigated and the information validated by Francis Story. Dr. Ian Stevenson did the same and wrote of them in his book, *Twenty Cases Suggestive of Reincarnation.*

Another example was documented in a program by Australian public television entitled "Reincarnation." Under hypnosis, Helen Pickering, who had never been out of Australia, remembered being Dr. James Burns of Scotland during the early nineteenth century, and she drew a picture of the medical college he had attended.

Later she traveled with the research team and two independent witnesses to the town where she remembered living. In the town records, a Dr. James Burns was mentioned as living there at the time she stated. Helen recognized the place where the pub had been, but commented how different it was now that it had been remodeled.

The researchers blindfolded her and drove to Aberdeen, the city where the medical college was. Once the blindfold was removed and Helen oriented herself, she led them without hesitation directly to the medical college. On the way, she told them where the old Seamen's Mission had been, and when town records were checked, this was validated.

Upon entering the medical college, she had a very strange feeling—it was clearly an emotional experience. Knowing exactly where she was going, she led the others around the college. At times Helen commented that the structure of the building had been different at the time of Dr. Burns, and when they consulted the local historian, this too was confirmed. The historian then asked her questions about the college and its floorplan as it had been nearly a century and a half before, and her answers were consistently correct. The witnesses and the historian, neither of whom believed in rebirth, were astonished and could only explain Helen Pickering's knowledge by the theory of rebirth.

## HOW DOES IT HAPPEN?

How does rebirth happen? What is it that is reborn? To understand this, we must first understand the nature of our body and mind, and what is meant by "life" in a spiritual, not biological, sense.

The term, "our mind," refers to each of our individual minds. The singular "mind" is used for stylistic purposes. Don't get confused, for we aren't parts of one big mind. Each of us has our own mindstream or mental continuum. Although in general "mind," "mindstream" and "mental continuum" are used interchangeably, the latter two terms emphasize the continuity of the mind over time.

Each of us has a body and a mind. While these two are together, we say, "I am alive." When they separate, we call it "death."

Our body and mind are different entities, each with its own continuum. Our body is material substance, a physical entity composed of atoms and molecules. We can see, hear, smell, taste, and touch it. We can examine sections of it under a microscope and analyze its chemical and electrical functions.

Our mind, however, is quite different. It's not the physical organ of the brain, but is that part of us that experiences, perceives, recognizes and emotionally reacts to our environment. Thus, "mind" doesn't refer to the intellect, but to the entire cognitive and experiential aspect of us, our consciousness. As it isn't composed of physical matter, our mind can't be measured by scientific instruments. We can't see, hear, smell, taste or touch our mind. While our body is atomic and physical in nature, the mind is formless and conscious.

In Buddhism, mind is defined as "mere clarity and awareness." It is clear in the sense that it reflects or illuminates objects. Objects—red roses, sweet fragrances, sounds and ideas—can all arise in the mind. The mind is aware in that it perceives or is involved with these objects. It knows or is aware of the world around and inside of us. The mind is this mere function of clarity and awareness, that which allows for the arisal of objects and is involved with them.

As neither psychology nor science have a concise definition of what mind or consciousness is, and since we tend to think of everything as having a molecular basis, it may seem strange at first to think of our consciousness as a formless entity. But if we sit quietly and let ourselves be aware of the qualities of clarity and awareness, we'll come to have a new understanding of what our mind is.

While we are alive, our body and mind are conjoined and affect each other. However, they are different entities. When we see a daisy, the neurons in our nervous system react in certain chemical and electrical patterns. However, neither the physical substances nor their chemical and electrical reactions is conscious of the flower. The eye sense organ, the nervous system and the brain are the physical bases allowing the mind to perceive and experience the daisy.

Our love for a dear one is a conscious experience. Although there are chemical and electronic reactions occurring in our nervous system at the time we're feeling love, the molecules themselves aren't experiencing that emotion. If love were only chemical functions, then we could create it in a petri dish! Thus, the chemical and electrical reactions aren't the love, although they may be occurring at the same time the consciousness is experiencing love.

Because the mind and body are separate entities, they each have their own continuum. Because the body is material and physical, its perpetuating cause—the thing that actually transforms into our body—is physical substance. Our body is a result of the sperm and egg of our parents. Similarly, what follows from our present body after death will also be physical in nature: a corpse which decomposes.

Our body functions within the system of cause and effect. Our body as it is today is dependent on the body we had yesterday. Although it's not made of exactly the same atoms as it was yesterday—our body took in food and eliminated waste—it still is a continuation of yesterday's body. We can trace the origin of our present body back to the fetus in the womb and eventually to the sperm and egg of our parents. The sperm and egg each have their own continuums, being produced by causes. Science hasn't identified a first moment of physical matter, and in fact, it's even questionable if such a first moment exists. Matter and energy change form, yet the total of the two neither decreases nor increases.

As the mind is mere clarity and awareness and not made of atoms, its perpetuating cause is also non-atomic and of the nature of clarity and awareness. Our present mind depends on our mind from yesterday. That depends on the mind of the day before, and so on: in this way we can trace back the continuation of our mind. Because our mind is a continuum that is constantly changing, we can experience new things each moment and we can remember what has happened to us in the past.

At a certain point, we can remember no further. Still, we know that we had consciousness as a baby because we can see that other babies have minds. Our mind when we were a baby was a continuation of our mind when we were a fetus, and so on back to the time of conception, each moment of mind being a result of the previous moment of mind.

At the time of conception, when the mind entered into the union of the sperm and egg, where did it come from? As we have seen, each moment of mind is a continuation of the previous moment. In the same way, the mind that joined with the fertilized egg was also a continuation of a previous moment of mind. It wasn't produced by the sperm and egg, because mind is a different entity from the material substances which constitute the body.

Buddhists believe that our mind was not created by another being or God, because consciousness cannot be created out of nothing. Furthermore, they say, why would a God create us? Surely there is no reason to create suffering or even create beings who have the potential to degenerate from perfection into suffering. Buddhists believe that if the cause is perfect, its result should also be; so the creation of a perfect God should be perfect. If created beings have the potential to degenerate, then they aren't perfect.

Because each moment of mind is a product of a previous moment, the only logical cause of the mind at the instant of conception is a previous moment in that same continuum. Thus, our mind existed prior to entering into this particular body. We have had previous lives, when our mind inhabited other bodies.

After death, although the physical matter of the body decays, the mind doesn't. The continuity of our mindstream takes rebirth in another body. Each moment of consciousness causes the next moment. Thus, because the cause (the moment of consciousness at the time of death) exists, the result (the next moment of consciousness) will exist. Our mindstream doesn't cease when the body ceases to function.

At the time of death our gross sense consciousnesses which enable us to see, hear, smell, taste and touch and our gross mental consciousness that thinks and conceives dissolve into an extremely subtle mental consciousness. This extremely subtle mental consciousness leaves our present body and enters an intermediate state.

The Buddha explained that in the intermediate state we take a subtle body similar to the gross physical one we'll take in the next rebirth. Within seven weeks all the causes and conditions for the future rebirth come together and we're reborn in another body. In this new body, all the gross consciousnesses again appear, and we see, hear, smell, taste, touch and think about our new environment.

When we're reborn, our mindstream joins with a new body. That is, we aren't reborn into a being that is already alive, since living beings already have mindstreams. At the beginning of this lifetime, our mind entered into the fertilized egg in our mother's womb. It didn't enter into a month-old baby, for that infant already had a mind.

Each person has a separate mindstream. We're not fragments of a "universal mind," because we each have our own experiences. That doesn't mean we're isolated and unrelated, for as we progress on the path we'll come to realize our unity and interdependence. Still, we each have a mindstream that can be traced back infinitely in time.

The very subtle consciousness that goes from one body to the next, from one life to the next, is not a soul. "Soul" implies a fixed, real and independent entity that *is* the person. The consciousness, however, is dependent and always changing, and thus is referred to as the mindstream.

A stream or river is constantly changing—sometimes it is narrow, other times wide; sometimes it flows peacefully in a broad valley, other times it gushes down over rocks and through gorges. What form the river takes downstream depends on what it was like upstream and on the conditions in the place down-stream. In spite of all the changes it goes through, a river—for example, the Mississippi—is one continuous thing, hav-ing the same name throughout its length.

In the same way, the mind or consciousness continuously changes. Sometimes it is peaceful, other times restless. Some-times it is in a human body, other times it is in other physical forms. What happens to our mind in one particular life de-pends on the actions it created and motivated in previous lives. Although our mind is constantly changing, like a river it is regarded as one continuous thing.

When did it all begin? From a Buddhist viewpoint, there is no initial moment of mind. Each moment of our mind arises because there is a cause for it, the previous moment of mind. There was no first moment. No one ever said there had to be a beginning, before which there was no mind. In fact, such a thing would be impossible, for how could a first moment of mind be created without the prior existence of its cause, a previous moment?

The idea of a beginningless regression may be difficult for us to grasp at first, but if we remember the numberline from math class, it'll be easier. Is there a highest number? Is there an end to the numberline on either the positive or negative side? To whatever we may name as the first or last number, one more can always be added. There is no beginning or end. It is similar with our mental continuum.

In fact, the Buddha said that it was fruitless to try to find a first moment of mind or the origin of our ignorance. We would waste our precious life in useless speculation about some-thing that didn't exist. It's more advantageous to deal with our present situation and work to improve it.

Why can't most of us remember our previous lives? This is because our minds are obscured by ignorance and the im-prints of negative actions we created in the past. But it's not surprising that we can't remember our previous lives: some-times we can't even remember where we put our keys, nor can we remember what we ate for dinner on February 5, 1970.

That we can't remember something doesn't mean it doesn't exist. It simply means that our memory is obscured.

People often ask where the "new" mindstreams come from as the population of the world increases. Buddhas and accomplished meditators who have purified their minds and developed single-pointed concentration have told of the existence of other life forms in the cosmos.

When beings living in other universes die, they can be reborn on our earth. After death, we can also be reborn in their worlds. Similarly, the animals around us may be reborn as humans. In this way, our human population on earth can increase.

From a Buddhist viewpoint, plants generally don't have minds. Although they are biologically alive in that they grow and reproduce, they generally aren't alive in the sense of having consciousness. While plants may react to their environment, it doesn't necessarily mean that they have minds, for even iron filings react when a magnet is brought near them. When we've cleared the ignorance and obscurations from our mindstreams, then we'll be able to distinguish directly which forms are sentient and which aren't.

## TRYING IT ON

Although we may not be thoroughly convinced of the existence of past and future lives, we can "try it on" in the sense of examining whether or not rebirth can explain other things that we previously didn't understand.

Parents often observe that their new-born infants have distinct personalities. One child in the family may be very quiet and content, while another is restless. One child may habitually lose his or her temper, while in the same situation another isn't irritated.

Why do such personality traits appear even at a very early age? Why are some of our personality traits very strong and ingrained? Certainly environmental and genetic influences are present. From a Buddhist viewpoint, other influences are present as well, for we don't seem to enter this life as blank slates.

We carry with us personality characteristics and habitual behavior patterns from previous lives.

Rebirth could explain why a particular child shows aptitude
from a very young age for music or math, for example. If we
are familiar with a certain subject or have developed a particular talent well in past lives, then an inclination towards it could
easily appear in this life. One woman told me that from a very
young age her son was interested in music and knew the names
of the composers of certain pieces. No one else in the family
had such knowledge or interest in music, and her son's af-
finity puzzled her. Perhaps the child was a musician in a previous life.

Many of us have had "deja vu" experiences when we've gone
to a place for the first time yet strongly feel that we've been
there before. This could be a subliminal recognition of a place
we've been to in a previous life.

Also, we've probably had the experience of meeting people
and feeling very drawn to them for no apparent reason. We
instantly feel relaxed and find ourselves discussing personal
issues with them. This could point to our having been close
friends in previous lives.

Most people need time to think over the various pieces of
evidence suggesting the existence of past and future lives. We
won't have a clear understanding of it at first and many questions are likely to arise. We need to learn, reflect upon and
discuss the evidence for and against rebirth. For some people, it requires courage to loosen the preconceptions they've
had since childhood and to investigate rebirth. But this is very
worthwhile: through examining issues with a mind open to
logic and evidence, our intelligence and understanding will
expand.

# 2  *Karma:*
## Cause and effect

*As a student of comparative religions, I believe that Bud-
dhism is the most perfect one the world has seen. The philosophy of the theory of evolution and the law of karma
are far superior to any other creed.*
　　　　　　　　*—Dr. C. G. Jung, Swiss psychologist*

What rebirth we take after leaving our body depends on our
previous actions. This is due to the functioning of cause and
effect: karma and its result. That is, what we do creates the
cause for what we'll become, and what we are now has come
about as a result of previously created causes.

Karma means action, and refers to the intentional actions
of our body, speech and mind: what we do, say and think.
These actions leave imprints and tendencies upon our mindstream. When these imprints and tendencies meet with proper
conditions, they affect what we experience.

The discussion of karma—actions and their results—is compatible with science and psychology. Physicists, chemists and
biologists research the functioning of cause and effect on a physical level. They investigate the causes producing a phenome-

non and the results occurring when certain things interact in a specific way. Psychologists look for the causes of mental disorders and the results that can come from certain treatments. Buddhism investigates cause and effect too, but in a more subtle way. It considers how cause and effect function on a subtle mental, not physical, level. In addition, Buddhism considers cause and effect over a series of lifetimes.

The fact that our experiences are results of our actions is not a system of punishment and reward. When a flower grows from a seed, it's neither a reward nor a punishment of the seed. It's merely a result. Similarly, when our actions bring our future experiences, these are results of our actions, not their rewards or punishments.

The Buddha didn't set down commandments, the infraction of which warrants punishment. As the Buddha has no wish for us to experience pain, he would never judge or condemn us. Our unpleasant experiences arise due to our own actions.

Newton didn't create the law of gravity; he merely described how it works. Similarly, the Buddha didn't create the system of cause and effect or karma. He described what he saw after having removed all obscurations from his mindstream.

We may think that it's unfair to experience in this life the result of what we did in previous lives. However, it's not really an issue of "fair" and "unfair." We don't say it's unfair that an object falls down and not up, for we know that no one invented gravity. Gravity isn't due to someone's favoritism. It's simply the way things naturally function. Similarly, no one made the rule that if we harm others now, we'll have problems in the future. This is simply the natural result arising from that cause.

Since we create the causes, we experience the results. The Buddha can't reach inside our minds and make us think or act differently. Since the Buddha has infinite compassion, if he were able to save us, he would have done so already. Our teachers can teach us the alphabet, but we must learn it. They can't learn it for us. Similarly, the Buddha described what to practice and what to abandon, but we must act on this. The Buddha can't do it for us.

The beauty of our human potential is that we are responsible for our own experience. Living in the present, we create our future. We have the ability to determine who we will be and what happens to us, and to ensure happiness for ourselves and others. To do this, we must assume our responsibility and use this ability.

## HOW CAUSE AND EFFECT WORK

There are four principal characteristics of cause and effect: (1) karma is definite, that is, positive actions are certain to bring happy results and negative actions definitely bring undesirable results; (2) karma is expandable: a small cause can bring a large result; (3) if the cause for a certain occurrence isn't created, that occurrence won't be experienced; and (4) the imprints our actions make on our mindstream don't get lost.

The first characteristic of karma is that constructive actions bring happy results and destructive ones bring unpleasant experiences. Actions aren't inherently good or bad in themselves, but are considered positive or negative according to whether they bring the result of happiness or pain. If apple seeds are planted, an apple tree will grow, but chili will not. Similarly, if positive actions are done, happiness will ensue, never pain. When suffering is experienced, it's caused by negative actions, never positive ones. The Buddha said:

> According to the seed that is sown,
> So is the fruit that you reap.
> The doer of good will gather good results,
> The doer of evil reaps evil results.
> If you plant a good seed well,
> Then you will enjoy the good fruits.

It's helpful to remember this in our daily life. For instance, suppose a person is tempted to lie in order to increase his profit in a business transaction. Then he remembers that this will bring unhappy results. Recognizing that although lying may bring temporary benefit, it will bring more problems in the long run, he decides not to lie. By avoiding lying, he reaps the long-term benefit of acting constructively as well as the short-term gain of winning others' trust and respect.

When misfortune occurs, some people react in anger, while others become depressed. Buddhist psychology focuses upon practical methods to extricate ourselves from such confusion and suffering. Thus, when we experience misfortune, it's helpful to remember that karma is definite. Rather than becoming emotionally upset, which only compounds our suffering, we can recall that this situation has arisen due to our own past actions.

For example, if our house is robbed, we suffer from losing our possessions. If, on top of that, we get angry, then we become even more miserable. However, when we consider that our possessions were stolen as a result of some past misdeed on our part—perhaps stealing or cheating others—it will be easier to accept what has happened without anger. By recognizing the undesirable effects arising from selfish actions, we'll have a firmer determination not to steal or cheat others in the future.

Some people react to misfortune by wallowing in self-pity: "I'm a terrible person. I deserve to suffer." It's more skillful to recognize that we experience unhappiness as a result of our past actions. This doesn't mean that we're "bad and worthless" people. It simply indicates we made mistakes in the past and are now experiencing their results. Accepting that we made mistakes and recognizing the problems that ensue, we can develop a firm intention to avoid creating the causes of suffering in the future.

Accepting that our problems are due to our own previous destructive actions doesn't mean we remain passive in the face of harmful situations. If we can do something to prevent or to correct a bad situation, we should do it! However, by remembering that this misfortune is due to our own destructive actions, we won't be angry or belligerent toward others as we try to remedy the problem.

The second characteristic of karma is that a small action can bring a large result. Just as a huge crop comes from a few seeds, a large result can come from a small action. Helping someone in a small way can result in great happiness, while harming someone slightly can bring years of misery.

Considering that small actions can bring large results helps us to stop rationalizing our negative behavior. Someone may think, "I just over-charged the customer a little bit," or "I only shouted at my family a short time." Of course, harming people a little is better than harming them a lot. Still, we can't dismiss it, for this action will bring its result. The imprint of an action gestates and produces a larger result.

Similarly, although we may not be able to do great constructive actions, it's important to do small ones, for even a small positive action can bring a great beneficial result. The seemingly small things in life are important. The Buddha said in the *Dhammapada*:

> Even small non-meritorious acts
> Can cause great ruin and trouble
> In the world that lies beyond—
> Like poison that has entered the body.

> Even small meritorious acts
> Bring happiness to future lives,
> Accomplishing a great purpose
> Like seeds becoming bounteous crops.

The third feature of karma is that if the cause hasn't been created, the result won't be experienced. This is quite logical: if no seed is planted, a crop doesn't grow. In a car accident, why is one person killed while another is not? Why does one person die of cancer at a young age, while another doesn't? This occurs because in previous lives, one person created the cause, the other one didn't.

Likewise, if we want happiness, we must create the cause for it. Just praying to be happy but not acting positively is like praying to know math but not studying it. If we don't create the cause, the result won't come. Awareness of this gives us enthusiasm to avoid harming and to act constructively.

Lastly, the imprints of our actions don't get lost. That is, unless a negative imprint is purified or unless a positive one is destroyed by anger or wrong views, it will eventually ripen when the proper conditions are assembled. Sometimes we lie and think, "It doesn't matter. No one knows about it. Nothing will happen." Actually, this isn't correct, for the imprints may remain on our mindstream a long time before circumstances become conducive for them to bear results. As the Buddha said in the *Dhammapada,*

> Whether it was good or bad,
> The power of any action
> Once performed is never lost;
> The results arise accordingly.

Some actions are destructive and undesirable by nature. These include killing, stealing, unwise sexual behavior, lying, divisive speech, harsh speech, idle talk, coveting others' possessions, maliciousness and wrong views. These ten destructive actions will be discussed further in the chapter on ethics. Avoiding these actions is in itself acting positively. Other positive actions include generosity, serving the sick and needy, helping our parents and teachers, consoling those who are grieving and otherwise being of service to others.

A general guideline for the actions to abandon and those to cultivate also can be established according to the motivation for the action. Actions motivated by attachment, anger, closed-mindedness, jealousy, pride and so on are negative actions. Those motivated by detachment, patience, compassion and wisdom are constructive. We have to look to the motivation of the action in order to determine whether the action itself is constructive or not, for without a particular intention, we don't speak or act.

Awareness of the role of motivation in determining the long-term results of our actions greatly helps in cutting through all hypocrisy and self-deceit. Sometimes we skillfully manipulate a situation so that we look good, even though our motivation is self-centered. For example, we may run an errand for a friend, not because we're sincerely interested in their welfare, but because we want them to feel obliged to us. In fact, there is no point in fooling ourselves, for the principal imprint made on our mindstream was a selfish one. Being aware of the results of such deceptive behavior helps us to examine our motivations honestly and correct those which aren't desirable.

## THE EFFECTS OF OUR ACTIONS

We don't necessarily experience the results of our actions immediately. When Susan loses her temper at her colleague Bill, she experiences the immediate result—he refuses to cooperate with her on the project they're doing that day. However, the result of her action doesn't stop there, but influences their relationship in the future as well. Even though she may be pleasant to him in the future, he will not trust her as much.

In addition, the imprints of her maliciousness and harsh speech remain on her mindstream and will influence her experiences in the future. Being in the habit of speaking harshly, she will easily repeat this action the next time the opportunity arises.

It would be a mistake to think that the results of our actions always come quickly and then cease. Just as it takes time for a seed to grow into a plant, it takes times for our karmic imprints to bring their results. As the Buddha said in the *Dhammapada*:

> Wrong actions do not necessarily
> Cut immediately like swords.
> Those who migrate through wrong actions
> Actualize the result afterwards.

Of course, the same applies for our positive actions. We may not instantaneously receive good results, but when the conditions come about for those constructive imprints to bring their results, they will. We should be satisfied to create positive causes and know that they'll ripen in the future. Being impatient for the result to come doesn't make it come quicker.

This is especially important to remember when we're engaged in a spiritual practice. Attaining enlightenment isn't like getting fast food! We tend to be impatient and want instant enlightenment. But if we think that we'll become enlightened after doing a little practice for a short time, we'll be disappointed. It takes time for our good imprints to ripen. Extended practice is needed to transform our minds.

An action that is complete with three parts, the motivation, the action itself, and the completion of the action, can influence four aspects of our experience: (1) the body we're born into in future lives; (2) what happens to us while we're alive; (3) our personality characteristics; and (4) the environment we live in.

First, our actions influence the type of body we're born into in future lives. Beneficial actions bring comfortable rebirths, while destructive actions bring uncomfortable ones. For example a good rebirth, such as the one we have now, is a result of constructive actions we did in previous lives. The imprints of previous positive actions attracted our mindstreams to be born as human beings in fortunate circumstances.

Similarly, if someone acts destructively—for example, his sexual behavior is reckless and inconsiderate—then a negative imprint is left on his mindstream. At the time of death, if he dies with much craving, this acts as a cooperative condition enabling the imprint of his destructive action to bring its result. His mind is attracted towards a body of an unfortunate life form. Because the causal action was destructive, the result will be an unfortunate rebirth.

Our previous actions affect what happens to us during our lifetimes. For example, if we're generous in one life, we'll experience prosperity in future lives. If we steal, in our future lives we'll face difficult economic conditions. It's very helpful to be mindful of this because it gives us a greater perspective on why things occur the way they do.

Our previous actions also influence our present personality characteristics. A person who habitually criticizes and abuses others will easily do so again in future lives. A person who has trained his or her mind in love and compassion will be inclined toward those traits in the future.

Some attitudes and reactions automatically arise within us. For example, some people are easily offended. Others are inclined to substance abuse. Some people are instinctively considerate of others. These various habitual reactions occur because we were familiar with these thoughts and actions in the past.

Although we're influenced by habitual negative tendencies from the past, these habits can be changed and new, more positive ones can be developed in their place. Also, it's advantageous to nurture our beneficial tendencies so they'll increase. In this way, we'll shape our personalities and improve our characters.

Finally, our actions influence the environment we are born into. In recent years people have become more aware of the influence of our actions on our environment. When we abuse the environment for our own selfish purposes, we harm ourselves. The greed for more profit leads humans to act in ways that directly damage our environment. Respecting life leads to restraint and consequently a more pleasant place to live.

Buddhist texts speak of the effect of our actions on the environment in another sense as well. For example, the scriptures say that acting destructively results in rebirth in an unpleasant environment, while acting constructively brings rebirth in pleasant surroundings and comfortable climates.

## PREDETERMINATION?

The functioning of cause and effect isn't predetermination. Nor is it fate. We have choice, if we're mindful and aware of our actions. If we're negligent and do, say and think anything that pops into our heads, then we aren't making use of our choice, we aren't taking advantage of our human potential.

Once an action is done, its result isn't cast in iron. Cause and effect means that things depend on each other. There is flexibility and we are able to influence to a certain extent how an imprint matures. For example, if we purify a negative action, we can prevent it from bringing its undesirable result. Conversely, if we become angry, we can destroy the potential of a positive action to bring its result.

The exact way in which a specific action ripens and what we did in the past to bring a specific result in our present life can only be known completely by a Buddha's omniscient mind. The Buddhist scriptures give general guidelines about the results of certain actions. However, in specific situations, the exact result may vary depending on other causes and conditions.

Whether an action brings a small or great result depends on the nature of the action itself, how it was done, who it's done to, the strength of the motivation, the frequency with which it's done, and whether it is regretted and purified later. All of these factors will influence the result. In addition, how the person dies affects which imprint matures and what result it brings. Thus, karma isn't rigid and fixed.

Suppose that Harry goes hunting and kills a deer. This action will definitely bring him suffering in the future. However, various other factors will affect what happens. Was he seriously intent upon staking out and killing the animal, or did he go hunting only with mild interest? Was Harry happy after killing the deer, or did he have some remorse? Did he purify the negative imprint left on his mindstream? Did he often kill animals? When Harry died, was he angry, or was he thinking of holy beings and their qualities? Did his friends and relatives do positive actions and prayers on Harry's behalf after he died? Such factors influence the specific result that comes from his action.

There are many nuances to every action. Only a Buddha has the complete ability to know exactly what specific past action or combination of actions brings a certain result in an individual's present life.

The natural law of karma isn't an excuse to avoid helping others. When witnessing others experiencing misfortune, some people may flippantly say, "Oh, that's their karma. If I help them, I'd be interfering with their karma." This is a misconception and a poor excuse for our own laziness. If we were hit by a car and lay bleeding in the road and a passer-by said, "Tsk, tsk, that's your karma. I'm not going to help you. You have to wear off your negative karma," how would we feel?

When others are in misery, we must help because they're living beings just like we are. In fact, if we don't help, we're creating the cause not to receive help when we need it. In Buddhist thought, we have a moral and social responsibility to help others. We aren't independent isolated individuals. Rather, we're inter-related and in spite of superficial differences, we're very similar.

Nor is the law of cause and effect a reason to look down on others. It's not correct to think, "The starving people in the world must have harmed others in the past. That's why they're suffering now. They're bad people and deserve what they get."

Such a judgmental attitude shows a lack of self-respect and implies that we too are evil people when we suffer. This is incorrect. If we examine our own lives, we know that sometimes our negative attitudes get the better of us. Although we may not want to scream at our family, our anger gets out of control and we do. Other times we may deliberately try to slander another and only later realize and regret what we've done. In neither instance would we like to be judged as "evil" or "bad." It's true that we made mistakes and will experience their painful results, but that doesn't mean we're evil individuals. Our disturbing attitudes simply overtook us at that moment.

Just as we have compassion for ourselves and want others to forgive us when we act destructively, so too should we have a forgiving attitude towards others. Resentment and revenge don't remove the harm done to us. They merely create more suffering for ourselves and others. Similarly, pride and condescension towards the unfortunate is inappropriate. When we have difficulties, we appreciate others' aid. Similarly, when others suffer misfortune, it's our human responsibility to help them as best we can.

When we see dishonest people who are wealthy or kind people who die young, we may doubt the law of cause and effect. However, cause and effect operate from one lifetime to another. Many of the results experienced in this life are results of actions created in previous lives, and many actions done now will ripen in future lives.

According to the Buddhist view, the wealth of dishonest people results from their generosity in previous lives. Their current dishonesty creates the cause for them to be cheated and impoverished in the future. Kind people who die young are experiencing the result of negative actions such as killing in past lives. However, their present kindness creates the imprints on their mindstreams for them to have happiness in the future.

## PURIFYING AND CHANGING

Certainly, all of us have made mistakes that we now regret. However, we aren't irrevocably condemned to experience the results of those actions. If a seed is planted in the ground, it will eventually grow, unless it's burnt or plucked out. In the meantime, we can postpone its growth by not giving it water, fertilizer and sunshine. Similarly, we can purify our negative actions so they won't bring painful results. If we aren't able to do that, we can postpone or weaken their effects. This is done by the purification process, which has four steps.

Purification by means of the four opponent powers is very important. It prevents future suffering and relieves the guilt or the heavy feeling we experience now. By cleansing our mind we're able to understand the Dharma better, are more peaceful and can concentrate better. The four opponent powers used to purify negative imprints are: (1) regret; (2) taking refuge and generating an altruistic attitude toward others; (3) performing an actual remedial practice; and (4) firmly determining not to do the action again.

First, we acknowledge and have regret for doing the destructive action. Self-recrimination and guilt are useless and are just a way of emotionally torturing ourselves. With sincere regret, on the other hand, we acknowledge that we made a mistake and regret having done it.

The second opponent power is that of reliance. Our destructive actions generally occur in relation to either holy objects such as Buddha, Dharma and Sangha, or other beings. To re-establish a good relationship with the holy objects we rely on them by taking refuge or seeking direction from them. To have a good relationship with other beings we generate an altruistic attitude and dedicate our heart to becoming a Buddha in order to be able to benefit them in the best way.

The third element is to actually do some remedial action. This could be any constructive action that benefits others. Buddhist texts outline some specific actions that help to cleanse negative imprints: listening to teachings, reading a Dharma book, paying homage to the Buddhas, making offerings, reciting the names of the Buddhas, chanting mantras, making statues or paintings of holy beings, printing Dharma texts, meditating and so on. The most powerful remedial action is to meditate on emptiness. How to do this will be explained in the chapter on wisdom.

Fourth, we determine not to act in such a way again. We frequently and habitually do some actions, like criticizing others or gossiping. It would be unrealistic to say we'll never do them again the rest of our lives. Therefore, it's wiser to choose a realistic amount of time and determine that we'll try not to repeat the action at all, but will be especially mindful and make a concerted effort during that period of time.

The four opponent powers must be applied repeatedly. We have acted destructively many times, so naturally we can't expect to counteract all those actions at once. The stronger the four opponents powers, the more powerful the purification will be. It's good to practice purification with the four opponent powers every evening before going to sleep. This counteracts whatever destructive actions we have committed during the day and helps us to sleep peacefully.

At present, our minds are like uncultivated fields. Purification is similar to taking away the rocks, bits of broken glass and bubblegum wrappers cluttering the field. Accumulating positive potential by acting constructively is similar to adding fertilizer and irrigating it. Then we can plant the seeds by listening to teachings and cultivate them through contemplation and meditation. After a while the sprouts of realizations will appear.

We must act to improve our lives and attain enlightenment. Although we can employ someone to clean our house and move in new furniture, we can't hire someone to clean our minds and install compassion and wisdom. However if we act, the beneficial results will surely follow.

# 3  Cyclic Existence:
## The ferris wheel of recurring problems

The situation in which we exist is called cyclic existence or
samsara in Sanskrit. It describes a cycle of recurring problems
in which we are continuously born, experience various problems during our lives and die. No external force or being keeps
us bound in cyclic existence. The source of our problems lies
in our own ignorance: we don't understand who we are or the
nature of phenomena around us.

According to Buddhist philosophy, because we're unaware
of our own nature we misunderstand our environment and ourselves. We think things exist in a way they don't. We have a
wrong conception of who we are, thinking we are a permanent, concrete, findable entity. Then, we cherish this illusory
"real self" dearly. The one thought in our minds from morning till night is, "I want happiness, and my happiness is the
most important." We think and act as if we were the center
of the universe, for the thought "my happiness, my suffering" is foremost and ever-present in our minds. Our concern
for others comes after our concern for ourselves.

Because we don't understand the ultimate nature of people
and phenomena, we develop attachment and anger towards
others. We cling to what benefits us; we have aversion to peo-

ple and things that seem to threaten our happiness. Our lives are spent in this cycle of likes and dislikes, wants and don't-wants. Our minds are like yoyos, emotionally rising and falling ceaselessly.

We also go up and down as we proceed from one life to the next. As we've acted both destructively and constructively during our lives, we sometimes are reborn in lives with much pain and at other times in lives with much happiness. Nothing is stable. There is no security, no guarantee that we will have continual happiness, even though that is what all of us want.

Under the influence of our ignorance we act and thus create karma. When we understand cause and effect, we try to act constructively. When we're ignorant in this regard or when we are careless, our minds easily fall under the influence of disturbing attitudes, such as attachment, anger, jealousy, pride, closed-mindedness, and we act negatively. These actions leave imprints on our mindstreams, and these imprints influence our experience.

At the time of death, our sense consciousnesses lose their ability to function and our mental consciousness becomes more and more subtle. This can be disconcerting because we're accustomed to living in our present bodies and are very attached to them. As we feel ourselves separating from our bodies at the time of death, we crave to remain in them. When we finally realize that separation is inevitable, we grasp for another body.

These two factors, craving and grasping, are the conditions causing the imprints of some of our previously created actions to mature. This causes our minds to be attracted to a particular life form, and we're reborn in another body. In this way, we go from one life to the next.

None of these rebirths is everlasting. We take these various bodies according to the causes we created, and we experience the result only as long as the causal energy to do so exists. Once that karma is exhausted, we leave that body to take another. Some of these rebirths may last a long time, but none of them lasts forever.

Some people have a very idealistic view about rebirth. They

think that after death we're somewhere in space. Looking down, we think, "Hmm, I want to be born to that mother and father." It's not like that. We don't consciously choose. By the power of our disturbing attitudes and actions, our mind-streams are propelled into another body. We find a body attractive, and we grasp to have it. In that way, we find ourselves in another life, and cyclic existence continues.

Some people think each rebirth is like a test: we are reborn into a particular situation to learn specific things. This view implies there is some hidden plan, that either someone else decides what we need to learn or we're aware of it ourselves. This isn't the case. We're born into a certain body because the causes and conditions for it have come together. There are no pre-planned lessons for us to learn in our lives. Whether or not we learn from our experiences is up to us.

## OTHER LIFE FORMS

According to Buddhist thought, there are six types of life forms in the cycle of constantly recurring problems. The three fortunate life forms are humans, semi-celestial beings and celestial beings. The three less fortunate ones are animals (including insects), life forms experiencing continual frustration and clinging, and life forms experiencing continual fear and pain. Some people have difficulty believing all six life forms exist because we can only see humans and animals. How can we know the others exist?

At the beginning of my Buddhist studies, I too found it difficult to believe in the existence of other life forms. Then I remembered that our senses aren't capable of perceiving everything which exists. Eagles can see things we humans can't; dogs can hear sounds we can't. We can't see atoms with our eyes, nor do we have comprehensive knowledge about other planets and solar systems. Acknowledging the limitation of our senses and the present scope of scientific knowledge, I began to think that other life forms could exist, but we aren't aware of them.

Another way that helped me to consider the possibility of the existence of other life forms was to observe the wide variety of moods, perceptions and behavior we have as human beings. For example, sometimes we are content, patient and forgiving. Due to our calm mental state, our environment and the people we encounter seem very pleasant and enjoyable. Even if someone tries to provoke us, we ignore it and by joking and chatting with him, have a good time.

Now, take that mental state, amplify it and project it outwards so it becomes our environment and body. This is the life form of a celestial being.

At other times, we are extremely angry and out of control. Sometimes our anger-energy is so great that although no one is bothering us, we look for someone to be angry at. Our anger is combined with paranoia and we become extremely sensitive and fearful without reason. How we perceive the people and things around us changes, and it appears that others are trying to harm us, even if they aren't. Imagine that angry, paranoid state of mind is intensified and projected outwards to become our body and environment. This is a life form of fear and pain.

In this way, we can imagine the existence of other life forms: our bodies and environments being manifestations of our mental states. Just as positive actions attract us toward fortunate rebirths, negative attitudes manifest unfortunate lives. Whatever we experience—happiness or misery—comes from our own minds.

Some people wonder why animals are included in the three unfortunate types of rebirth. Some animals are intelligent and kind. Some live in better conditions than some humans. Seldom are animals as destructive as humans potentially can be. Animals only kill when it's necessary; they don't manufacture atomic bombs that can destroy civilization.

These points are well taken. Nevertheless, humans have a particular potential and intelligence that if used wisely can bring far greater results than those of an animal. A cat can't understand our advice to stop killing mice and to have compassion for them, nor can a dolphin comprehend the teachings on the ultimate nature of phenomena. In comparison, our human lives are special in that it's comparatively easy for us to avoid negative actions and to do positive ones.

Although animals are considered to have a lower rebirth, that doesn't mean humans should exploit and abuse them. On the contrary, Buddhism says all life forms should be respected, cared for and treated properly.

How can those reborn as animals become humans again? In previous lives, when they were humans, they acted both positively and negatively. The imprints of all these actions remain on their mindstreams. At the end of that human life, a negative imprint matured and caused the person to be born as an animal.

It's difficult for animals to cultivate positive attitudes and to act according to them. However, animals can receive positive imprints from hearing prayers and recitations of Dharma texts or from walking around Buddhist monuments or temples. Due to contact with a powerful virtuous object, a beneficial imprint is made on their minds. This is similar to the imprint made when "Eat popcorn" is flashed on a movie screen. We aren't aware of it, yet it has an impact on our minds.

Animals' mindstreams retain the positive imprints created while they were human. When the karmic energy to be animals finishes—rebirth in both the lower and upper realms is temporary, not eternal—then it's possible for positive imprints to mature, causing them to again be born as human beings.

With compassion, the Buddha described the existence of the various life forms in order to make us aware of the possible long-term effects of our actions. Knowing this, we'll be mindful of what we think, say and do, and we'll take the time to develop our good qualities. The Buddha observed:

> Sufferings originate from nowhere else but our own untamed minds. If we wish to achieve a true state of happiness, the best way is to train ourselves to eliminate our negative states of mind.

# PART IV

# OUR POTENTIAL FOR GROWTH

# 1 *Buddha Nature:*
## Our inborn goodness

We've seen that our situation is one of constantly recurring problems. We've also determined its causes: ignorance, the disturbing attitudes it gives rise to and the actions motivated by these disturbing attitudes. Now we may wonder, "Can people who are confused, attached and angry ever attain Buddhahood? Is there a way out of cyclic existence? If so, what is it?"

Yes, it is possible to free ourselves from this cycle of constantly recurring problems. We can attain a state of lasting peace and joy, in which we're able to utilize all our good qualities for the benefit of others. This is possible because we have within us the Buddha nature, our indestructible goodness. In addition, we have precious human lives which give us the opportunity to actualize our Buddha nature. These are the topics of the next two chapters.

Have you ever stood on a mountain and looked at a completely clear and empty sky? The feeling of space, calm and clarity is awesome and inspiring. But when we peer up at the sky from the middle of a city, our view is limited by the highrises around us, and we can't see the sky because the clouds and pollution obscure it. From the point of view of the sky, nothing has changed. The sky is still pure, empty and filled with light. However, we aren't able to see it; our outlook is narrow and the sky is obscured by the clouds and smog.

The nature of our minds is similar. Ultimately, it's pure and undefiled. The clouds that prevent us from seeing this real nature of our minds are the disturbing attitudes like attachment, anger and ignorance, as well as the imprints of the actions done under their influence.

The sky and the clouds aren't the same entity. They aren't inseparably united. The clouds and pollution are temporary obscurations which can be dispelled, revealing the clear, empty sky. Similarly, our disturbing attitudes and the imprints of the actions created by them are not the ultimate nature of our minds. They can be purified and removed forever, letting us perceive and be unified with our own spacious nature.

How do we know the disturbing attitudes and imprints of actions are not the nature of our minds? If anger, for example, were the nature of our minds, we would always be angry. But that is not the case: our anger comes and goes. The karmic imprints are also not the nature of our minds because they can be purified and removed.

Is it possible to eliminate our anger forever? Yes, it is, because anger is a false mind, an attitude based on a misconception. Anger is generated when we project negative qualities onto people and things. We misinterpret situations so they appear harmful to us. Absorbed in our own projections, we mistake them for the qualities of other people and get angry at what we ourselves have superimposed on them. The tragedy is that we're not aware of this process, and mistakenly believe the rude, insensitive person we're perceiving really exists out there.

Through the development of wisdom, we'll come to recognize that an external enemy is an exaggerated projection of our own mistaken minds. At this time, our anger will automatically vanish, for wisdom and ignorant anger can't be manifest at the same time. Through constantly developing our wisdom we can totally eliminate our anger.

Disturbing attitudes such as anger, jealousy and conceit are based on the faulty foundation of wrong projections and thus can be eliminated. Positive qualities such as patience, love, and compassion have a valid basis, because they recognize the good qualities all other beings have. Thus, such attitudes can never be extricated from our mindstreams. Rather, they can be developed limitlessly.

Each being has the possibility to become a Buddha because each of us has two kinds of Buddha potential. One is the ultimate nature of our minds, the way in which our minds exist. This phenomenon is a negation, an absence or lack of our minds existing in fantasized ways. The other is an affirmative phenomenon. It is the conventional nature of our minds, the qualities of our minds.

The ultimate nature of our minds is called the natural Buddha potential. It's like pure and vast empty space. That is, our ultimate nature is empty of all fantasized ways of existence. It's empty of all false projections of being unchanging or independent. Our minds are free from inherent existence. This will be explained in the chapter on wisdom.

The ultimate nature of our minds is untainted by the disturbing attitudes. It's without beginning or end. Nothing can destroy it. No one can take it away from us. This empty nature of our minds is our birthright. Knowing this, we'll have self-confidence, for we can become Buddhas.

At the moment our natural Buddha nature is obscured by the disturbing attitudes. As we clear them away through practicing the path, our Buddha nature will become more apparent to us.

The second type of Buddha potential is the evolving Buddha potential. This includes both the conventional nature of our minds—their clarity and awareness—and the positive mental states such as compassion.

The mind is a formless entity, not composed of atoms or material substance. It's clear in that it illuminates or makes objects clear. It's aware because it has the ability to cognize or perceive objects.

Both anger and compassion are states of mind and thus are

clear and aware. This nature of clarity and awareness is one of our evolving Buddha potentials. However, anger itself isn't part of our Buddha potential because it's based on false conceptions that can be eliminated.

Compassion, on the other hand, isn't based on false projections and thus can be developed infinitely. Similarly, the other mental states that perceive things accurately—love, patience, confidence, non-attachment, consideration for others, joyous effort and so on—can be increased limitlessly. These good qualities, existing in us at this present moment, will evolve as we follow the path. At the end of the path, they'll transform into the minds of the Buddhas that we'll become. For this reason, they're also called the evolving Buddha nature. The great Indian logician and sage, Dharmakirti, said:

The nature of the mind is clear light.
The obscurations are temporary.

Dharmakirti is reaffirming our possibility to become Buddhas by asserting that the nature of our minds is clear light. This has two meanings, corresponding to the two types of Buddha potential. First, our minds are clear light in that they are empty of all fantasized ways of existence. When our wisdom directly perceives this clear light, the emptiness of inherent existence, then we're capable of totally eliminating our disturbing attitudes from their root.

Second, our minds are clear light because their nature of clarity and awareness is always there. Our disturbing attitudes and karmic imprints aren't mixed with this clear and cognizing nature of our minds. In other words, we aren't our anger; we aren't our bad qualities. These are obscurations that can be removed.

The topic of Buddha nature is a profound one, so we may not understand it well at the beginning. But we can get a sense of our inner potential and inner beauty, our Buddha nature which is temporarily obscured by the clouds of anger, attachment and other disturbing attitudes. As we start removing the clouds, the meaning of our two Buddha natures will become clearer. The *Hevajra Tantra* says:

> Sentient beings are just Buddhas
> But they are obscured by temporary stains.
> When those are removed, they are Buddhas.

The first line doesn't mean we are already Buddhas, for then we would be ignorant Buddhas! It means we have the two types of Buddha nature. When we clear away the obscurations from our mindstreams, the continuation of our present minds transforms into the minds of the Buddhas we will become.

Thus, Buddhism takes a very positive and optimistic view of life and of human nature. Each of us has within us the seeds of perfection, the natural and evolving Buddha potentials, and these seeds can be neither stolen or destroyed. There is no reason for us to ever feel hopeless and helpless. Because our Buddha potential is inseparably within us, there is always a basis for self-confidence and positive aspiration.

At the moment, our Buddha potential is dormant within us, covered by the clouds of our disturbing attitudes and karmic imprints. Sometimes our Buddha potential is compared to honey surrounded by angry bees, or pure gold wrapped in impurities. The bees and the impurities, just like our disturbing attitudes and the imprints of actions, are temporary obscurations.

How do we remove them? By following the path described by the Buddha: cultivating wisdom and compassion. The wisdom realizing emptiness enables us to perceive our natural Buddha potential, which is empty of fantasized ways of existence. Compassion is a realistic attitude wishing everyone to be free from all unsatisfactory and miserable conditions. Determining to be free from our constantly recurring problems is the first step of the path. It sets the stage for developing our compassion and wisdom, thus allowing our Buddha potential to blossom. We can learn the techniques to purify and develop our minds by studying the teachings of the Buddha.

## 2  *Our Precious Human Life:*
Using a good opportunity

At times we may become depressed because it seems our lives have no direction or there are many obstacles to making our lives meaningful. However, when we consider the freedom and opportunities we have, we'll be amazed and filled with joy. We'll understand that depression is in fact fueled by a narrow view. When we recognize our opportunities we'll automatically feel happier.

As human beings, we have the intelligence to understand our world. In spite of the ways humans may sometimes misuse their intelligence, the potential to use it in beneficial ways exists. Technological and material progress aren't the only ways to make use of our human potential. Although technology has solved many problems, it's also created new ones. Some countries have high standards of living, yet their citizens aren't perfectly happy. They still suffer from social and mental ills, worries and conflicts.

This occurs because the basic cause of our difficulties—our ignorance, anger and attachment—haven't been removed. As long as we have these disturbing attitudes we won't be content, no matter how luxurious our environment. Thus, from a Buddhist perspective, the most beneficial way to use our intelligence is to develop altruism and wisdom knowing our ultimate nature. When our minds are peaceful, we'll be happy wherever we are. In addition, we'll be able to create a more peaceful environment.

Unfortunately, most humans—ourselves included—aren't aware of our potentials and consequently don't develop them. We often take our human intelligence for granted. Sometimes we're dismayed because some people misuse their intelligence. However, as we realize how our intelligence can make our lives and others' happier, then we'll be energetic, joyful and inspired to make use of our capabilities.

Not only are we human, but most of us have our senses intact. We're able to see and hear, which gives us great access to information and enables us to learn easily about the gradual path to enlightenment. Moreover our brains function well, so we have a great capacity to learn, think and meditate. So often we take these qualities for granted, but if we considered what it would be like to have impaired hearing, sight or intelligence, we would realize how fortunate we are.

This isn't to say that blind and deaf people can't progress along the path to enlightenment. They certainly can, for they have the two kinds of Buddha nature. However, it's easier to learn the Dharma when our senses are intact. Those of us who can see and hear well should appreciate our good fortune.

In addition, we live in a world where the Buddha's teachings exist. Not only did the Buddha describe the path, but his teachings have been practiced and passed down for over 2,500 years in unbroken transmissions from teacher to student until the present day. If the Buddha's teachings had been destroyed by political suppression or distorted by those seeking fame and wealth, we would no longer be able to practice them. However, that didn't occur, and today we have access to many Buddhist traditions.

There have been and still are many great masters who have actualized the realizations of the path. Their experience proves that liberation and enlightenment can be achieved and that the path taught by Shakyamuni Buddha brings the results we desire. Also, many great spiritual teachers are alive today, and they can guide us and act as good examples.

We're fortunate to live in a place where we can contact spiritual teachers and teachings. We have religious freedom, so we can learn and practice our faith. Imagine how terrible it would be to have an intense wish to develop ourselves, but to live in a country without religious freedom! Now we have the opportunity to go to Buddhist centers, learn meditation, listen to talks and do retreats. We have access to qualified teachers, as well as books, cassettes, videos and transcripts of Buddhist talks.

From our side, we're interested in personal development and in making our lives meaningful for others. This openness is a positive quality we should appreciate about ourselves. Many people don't have such inclinations and never examine what life and death are about. Even though what they seek is happiness, their lives are usually spent creating destructive actions, the causes of future unfortunate circumstances. Because they were never interested in eliminating their obscurations and developing their potentials, such people die with worry and regret. Although we can't confidently say our lives are in order and our own minds peaceful, we can appreciate that we have the interest and inclination to grow in this direction.

Some people may have such inclinations, but lack the material and financial conditions to pursue their spiritual goals. If we were starving, homeless and destitute, it would be more difficult for us to practice, for we would have to see to our physical condition first. However, most of us have a relatively comfortable material situation in which we can learn and practice. Although we may feel we aren't financially secure, if we compare our situation with that of others, we'll realize that we're very fortunate indeed.

We should realize that we live near others who have similar inclinations for self-development and service to others. These spiritual friends are a great support for our practice, for we can discuss what we learn and share experiences with them. This is both delightful and necessary, for sometimes we become discouraged or unclear, and our Dharma friends help to rekindle our energy. We are fortunate to have such friends, or to live in a place where we can meet them.

In addition, the Sangha communities of ordained monks and nuns give us good examples to follow. Although we may not want to have the same lifestyle they do, we can benefit from their example and their experience and knowledge of the path.

If we take a moment and evaluate the good circumstances we have in this lifetime, we'll be amazed and joyful. It's important to consider the advantages of our present situation, because then we'll stop taking them for granted and will use them. If we only think about our obstacles and what we lack, we spiral into depression. Depression prevents us from using our good qualities, as we don't recognize them and are too immersed in self-pity. This is a sad waste of human potential. It is counteracted by remembering our good qualities and opportunities.

Whether our gold-like Buddha potential stays embedded in the impurities of disturbing emotions and imprints of actions, whether the spacious nature of our minds remains invisible behind the clouds of our obscurations, is dependent on us. This is the beauty of our human life: we have the indestructible Buddha potentials which have been with us since beginningless time, and we have the perfect opportunity to realize and develop them in this lifetime. With great compassion, the Buddha taught the Dharma, the methods to actualize our potentials. We have the support and help of the Sangha to guide us. But we ourselves must act. Only then will we progress on the path to happiness.

## USING OUR LIVES TO FOLLOW THE PATH

There are various ways to use our lives to progress along the path to happiness. Although we all want to be happy now, when we push and grasp for that happiness, it evades us. On the other hand, if we're content with what we have and simultaneously prepare for the future, we'll be happier now and in the future.

One way to progress along the path is to practice moment by moment in our daily activities. When we wake up, instead of thinking, "What do I have to do today?" or "I want a cup of coffee," we can make our first thought of the day, "As much as possible, I'm not going to harm others today. As much as possible, I'm going to help them." It's a simple thought, but starting the day this way revolutionizes how we live. This thought to cherish others and refrain from harming them gives us a positive motivation and a clear direction in all the day's activities. If we encounter a disturbing situation during the day, we can remember our morning motivation. That helps us to act beneficially and to avoid anger, pride and jealousy.

In addition, throughout the day, we can cultivate the motivation, "I'm going to act for the benefit of others. I aspire to diminish my limitations and develop my potentials completely in order to be able to help others most effectively." In this way, we can transform otherwise insignificant actions into the path to enlightenment. An action can be done at different times with different motivations. According to our motivation, we'll be happy or unhappy and our action will be worthwhile or not.

For example, we can reluctantly clean the house, all the time wishing this unpleasant work was done so we could do something enjoyable. In this case, we're not very happy now, and our action of cleaning is neutral, neither constructive nor destructive. On the other hand, if we think, "It would be nice to clean the house so my family can enjoy a pleasant environment," then we're happy to vacuum and sweep. In addition, if we imagine that we're cleaning the dirt of the disturbing attitudes from the minds of all living beings, then mopping the floor can become a meditation! In this way our action becomes constructive, and a positive imprint is left on our mindstream.

By generating a good motivation in the morning and reflecting on it throughout the day, we'll find our wish to help others and not harm them arises more easily and becomes more heartfelt. The path to enlightenment is a slow and gradual one that's developed day by day. Each morning is a new opportunity to cultivate our good qualities, and each moment of the day is a chance to live them.

A second way to use our lives to follow the path is to prepare for death and our future lives. Although some people hesitate to think about death, it's beneficial to do so, for then we can prepare for it. Thinking that someday we'll die isn't being morbid, it's being realistic. Death is fearful only when we don't have a method to relate to it properly.

However, if we know how to prepare for death and what to do when it occurs, then it needn't be frightening. In fact, it could be very blissful. If we make our lives beneficial now, we'll have nothing to regret when they end. We'll be able to die peacefully and happily.

The basic method to prepare for death and future lives is to avoid destructive actions and do constructive ones. This refers particularly to avoiding the ten negative actions (see the chapter on ethics), and living according to ethical values. It also includes cultivating loving kindness towards others and doing whatever we can to help them.

The third way to make our lives meaningful is more expansive. While initially we prepare for future lives, we'll now aim for liberation from the cycle of uncontrolled rebirths and their constantly recurring problems. Beyond that, we can attain the full enlightenment of a Buddha, in which all obscurations have been eliminated and all good qualities fully developed. Liberation is attained by practicing ethical conduct, meditative concentration and wisdom (also called the three higher trainings). When these are combined with the altruistic intention to attain enlightenment in order to benefit all beings, then enlightenment is reached.

These may seem like lofty goals, but we have the opportunity to attain them. We sometimes underestimate what we can do and unnecessarily limit our goals. When we consider that all the past great masters and people whom we admire had precious human lives like ours, then we'll acknowledge our own potential to accomplish what they did. It's important that we recognize our potential and rejoice in it. As the Indian practitioner Aryadeva said:

> When we obtain a precious human rebirth, we gain the incredible ability not only to free ourselves from the suffering of cyclic existence forever, but also to gain the state of enlightenment, liberating countless beings from suffering. There is nothing to compare with this precious human rebirth. Who would waste such a rebirth?

By taking advantage of our great opportunity, we'll experience the blissful results of improving ourselves. We'll attain a state completely free of all problems, in which we'll be able to benefit all other beings by showing them the path to happiness through actualizing their own Buddha potentials.

| THREE WAYS TO USE OUR PRECIOUS HUMAN REBIRTH TO FOLLOW THE PATH | |
| --- | --- |
| Goal along the path | Method to accomplish it |
| 1. To make our lives meaningful moment by moment | Develop an altruistic motivation each morning; be mindful of our actions during the day; transform all events into opportunities for growth. |
| 2. To die peacefully and attain a good rebirth | Live ethically: avoid destructive actions and cultivate beneficial actions. |
| 3. To attain lasting happiness<br>  a. liberation from cyclic existence | Practice the three higher trainings: ethics, concentration and wisdom. |
|   b. full enlightenment (Buddhahood) | Practice the three higher trainings and the six far-reaching attitudes—generosity, ethics, patience, joyous effort, meditative stabilization and wisdom—with an altruistic motivation. |

# PART V

# THE PATH TO ENLIGHTENMENT

# 1   The Four Noble Truths:
## Teachings of the realized beings

*The message of the Buddha is a message of joy. He found a treasure and he wants us to follow the path that leads us to the treasure. He tells man that he is in deep darkness, but he also tells him that there is a path that leads to light. He wants us to arise from a life of dreams into a higher life where man loves and does not hate, where man helps and does not hurt. His appeal is universal, because he appeals to reason and to the universal in us all: 'It is you who must make the effort. The Great of the past only show the way.' He achieved a superior harmony of vision and wisdom by placing spiritual truth to the crucial test of experience; and only experience can satisfy the mind of modern man. He wants us to watch and be awake, and he wants us to seek and to find.*
*—Juan Mascano, Spanish academic and educator,*
*lecturer at Cambridge University*

The first teaching given by the Buddha described his realization in terms of four facts about existence, known as the Four Noble Truths. These four truths are: (1) We undergo undesirable experiences (the truth of suffering). These unsatisfactory experiences are to be identified. (2) These experiences have causes: ignorance and disturbing attitudes (the truth of the cause). These causes are to be abandoned. (3) There exists a peaceful situation in which all these undesirable experiences and their causes have been eliminated (the truth of cessation). The cessation of each disturbing attitude is to be actualized. (4) There's a path which will lead us to this state of peace (the truth of the path). The path is to be practiced.

## IDENTIFYING UNDESIRABLE CONDITIONS

Translating the first fact as "the truth of suffering" can be misleading, for the term "suffering" connotes great pain. Thus when we hear that the Buddha said life was suffering, we wonder what he was talking about, for most of us don't experience extreme misery most of the time. Actually, the Pali and Sanskrit term *dukha* connotes that things aren't completely right in our lives. Something is amiss; there are unsatisfactory conditions in our existence.

Most of us would agree with this. We know from our own experience that when we talk to people, be they rich or poor, leaders or followers, for more than five minutes, they'll inevitably start to tell us about problems in their lives. Everybody has some difficulty, something that isn't going well in his or her life.

We experience unsatisfactory situations: we don't get what we want, or we get what we don't want. While we have to work hard to obtain what we like, what we don't like comes effortlessly, without our having to ask or work for it! Even when we get things we desire, they don't last forever. Our possessions break or go out of style. We can't always be with the people we love. Eventually our most cherished relationships end, either through separation or death.

Besides these problems, there is the basic situation of being born, getting sick, growing old and dying. The very nature of our bodies is that they become sick: who can we point to who has never been sick? Also, without choice, we grow old.

From the time we're born we are aging. There's no way to stop time, nor can face-lifts or body building prevent the natural process of growing old. The only thing we can say will definitely happen to us in our life is that we will die, for no one can avoid death.

None of these situations is particularly appealing, is it? We try to make our lives fantastic and exciting in superficial ways: we create shopping malls, Disneyland, the Miss Universe contest, company banquets, family reunions and so on. Nevertheless, when we're honest with ourselves, we have to admit our situation isn't one hundred percent okay. We continually feel something is missing, and we search for more and better.

The Buddha didn't describe these problems and difficulties in order to make us depressed. They exist whether or not we think about them. However, by recognizing the unsatisfactory nature of our experience, we can then work to change it. The Buddha discussed suffering to motivate us to change our unsatisfactory experiences. The Buddha likened our present condition to that of a person suffering from a severe illness. Pretending there's no illness doesn't make the disease go away. That person must first admit she's sick and seek a doctor's advice. Then she can be cured by taking medicine. The same is true in life. Although initially we may not want to think about our unsatisfactory situation, doing so propels us to seek solutions. In addition, we may feel relieved by being honest with ourselves. Seeing that we can make things better, we become encouraged and invigorated.

## CAUSES TO BE ABANDONED

To change the situation, we must eliminate its causes: disturbing attitudes such as ignorance, anger and attachment. When these arise in our minds, we're unhappy, and we act in ways that make others unhappy. These actions create the causes for ourselves to experience unpleasant situations now and in the future.

Disturbing attitudes can be eliminated, for they rest on the foundation of ignorance. If we follow the path of ethical conduct, concentration and wisdom, we'll be able to eliminate the disturbing attitudes and their unpleasant results once and for all. Having done so, we'll be free to abide in a state of peace and bliss. This path has been seen as true by the noble ones who have actualized it in their own mindstreams, and the resulting blissful freedom is their own experience.

## THE CESSSATION OF PROBLEMS IS PEACE

The state of peace, in which the disturbing attitudes, actions and the problems they generate cease, is called liberation or nirvana. The person who has attained this is called an arhat. If we go even further and purify all subtle obscurations and develop all our qualities, then we'll attain enlightenment, the state of a Buddha.

Some people ask, "Isn't nirvana boring? Don't we need suffering to know what happiness is?" The answer is no. Boredom is a function of ignorance and attachment, and since these have been eliminated when we attain liberation, we no longer get bored. Also, we have experienced suffering already; we don't need to continue to have it in order to recognize happiness.

In the state of nirvana, our minds are peaceful, concentrated and wise. People who have attained nirvana aren't spaced-out and inactive. Rather, they possess great inner resources and radiate a sense of freedom and bliss.

## THE PATH TO PEACE

How can we attain liberation and enlightenment? By following the path leading to those goals. There are many ways to explain this path. One is in terms of the noble eightfold path—the practice of correct action, speech, livelihood, mindfulness, concentration, effort, view, and thought. To avoid making this book too long, the noble eightfold path isn't explained in detail. There are many excellent books on this subject, some of which are listed at the end of this book.

---

### THE FOUR NOBLE TRUTHS

1. The truth of undesirable experiences

2. The truth of the causes of these experiences — disturbing attitudes / karmic actions

3. The truth of cessation of undesirable experiences and their causes

4. The truth of the path to peace

---

Another way to describe the path is by speaking of three principal realizations: the determination to be free, the altruistic intention to attain enlightenment for the benefit of all beings, and the wisdom realizing reality. These three are called realizations because as we familiarize ourselves with them, these deep understandings become part of us and transform our outlook on the world. We'll discuss these three principal realizations in the next few chapters.

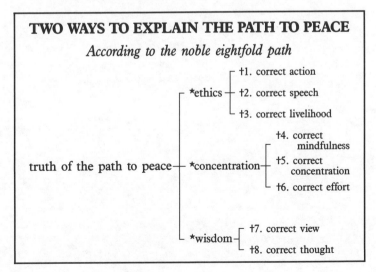

### TWO WAYS TO EXPLAIN THE PATH TO PEACE

*According to the noble eightfold path*

truth of the path to peace

- \*ethics
  - †1. correct action
  - †2. correct speech
  - †3. correct livelihood
- \*concentration
  - †4. correct mindfulness
  - †5. correct concentration
  - †6. correct effort
- \*wisdom
  - †7. correct view
  - †8. correct thought

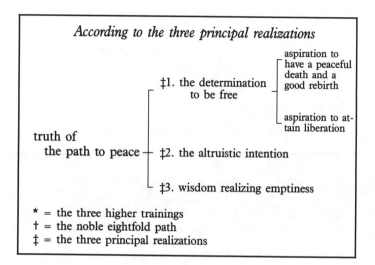

*According to the three principal realizations*

truth of
  the path to peace

‡1. the determination to be free

    aspiration to have a peaceful death and a good rebirth

    aspiration to attain liberation

‡2. the altruistic intention

‡3. wisdom realizing emptiness

★ = the three higher trainings
† = the noble eightfold path
‡ = the three principal realizations

## 2 *The Determination to be Free:* Developing the courage to free ourselves from a bad situation

The first principal realization of the path is the determination to be free from all problems and dissatisfaction. This arises from recognizing that our present situation isn't completely satisfactory and that we're capable of experiencing greater happiness. Thus, we'll determine to free ourselves from a bad situation and to aim for a better one.

Some people use "renunciation" to mean the determination to be free. This is a misleading term because renunciation suggests self-mortification and asceticism. In fact, that isn't the meaning of the Sanskrit and Pali term.

The determination to be free is an attitude. It doesn't mean we have to leave our family and job to go live in a cave and eat nettles! The determination to be free is a call to change our attitude. The lifestyle we choose is another matter.

In other words, what we appear to be externally isn't important, but what we are internally is. Living an ascetic life doesn't necessarily mean that one has no interest in worldly pleasures: one could live in a cave and still daydream about food or sports cars! Material possessions and other people aren't the problem. The problem is how we relate to them.

There are two levels to the determination to be free. The first is to be free from difficulties in future lives and to have happy rebirths. The second is to be free from all uncontrolled rebirth in cyclic existence and to attain liberation.

Why should we prepare for future lives? What about this life? There are a few reasons. First, preparing for future lives automatically makes our present life happier. To create the causes for happiness in future lives, we need to live ethically. When we avoid killing, stealing, unwise sexual behavior, lying, slander, harsh words, idle talk, coveting, maliciousness and wrong views, we'll naturally become kinder people. We'll get along better with others, and they'll like and trust us more because we've stopped harming them. Also, we'll be free from regret and guilt and will have a greater sense of inner purpose.

Second, preparing for the future isn't something unusual. Most people prepare for their old age, in spite of the fact that many never live that long. On the other hand, preparations for future lives will never go to waste, because our minds continue after death.

Third, our present lives may not last long, and our future lives may begin soon, for we don't know how long we'll live. Also, since our present lives are short compared to the duration of the many lives to come, it's wise to prepare for future lives.

## THE DISADVANTAGES OF ATTACHMENT

Attachment, an attitude which exaggerates the good qualities of a person or thing and clings to it, is the chief impediment to developing the determination to be free. Most of us are primarily concerned only with the happiness of our present life. We seek happiness by gratifying our senses. We always want to see beautiful things or nice-looking people, hear nice music or pleasing words, smell pleasant odors, taste delicious food and touch pleasing objects. We continually divide the world into what is attractive and what is repellent. We're attached to what we consider pleasant and have aversion towards anything we deem unpleasant. With such a limited outlook, our minds have no space to consider future lives' happiness or the bliss of liberation.

Ironically, seeking the happiness of only this life brings the opposite effect. To secure the objects of our attachment and to be free from those we have aversion for, we may act negatively and selfishly. These destructive actions create immediate problems as well as lay imprints on our mindstreams that will generate unpleasant experiences in future lives.

For example, why do we angrily criticize other people? Attached to our own happiness, we lash out at those who seem to obstruct it. At that moment, we don't care if we hurt their feelings. Sometimes we criticize others to feel powerful or to retaliate. When we succeed in harming them, we're happy: "I got even! They're miserable!" But what kind of people are we when we rejoice and gloat over others' misery?

When we act negatively, we get very confused. If we steal, we don't feel comfortable with ourselves. We can't sleep well and are anxious that the authorities might investigate our affairs. If we engage in extramarital affairs, we become worried, and lie and make excuses to cover up. The relationship with our spouse deteriorates and mistrust grows. Our children suspect something is wrong, and feel insecure and upset. They lose respect for us. In addition to the problems such activities create now, they leave imprints on our mindstreams that cause us to encounter unhappy situations in the future.

When we're very attached to the happiness of this life, we tend to exaggerate the importance of certain things. For example, we think, "I have to earn such and such a salary in order to be happy." Until we earn that much, we feel unfulfilled. We overestimate the importance of money, and ignoring all the other good things in our life, become obsessed with accumulating it. Even if we get it, our attachment brings new problems: we fear others will steal our money or worry that people are friendly to us only because we're rich. If the stock market goes down, we're depressed.

The disadvantages of attachment were discussed extensively in the chapters "Taking the Ache out of Attachment" and "Love vs. Attachment," so they won't be repeated here. It must be emphasized, however, that the Buddha didn't say sensual objects are bad or wrong. He encouraged us to examine our own experiences to determine whether or not sensual pleasures really bring the happiness we think they do. Also, he stressed that the problem lies not in the objects of the senses themselves, but in our attachment to them.

Without true understanding we may verbally pay tribute to the idea that attachment to sensual pleasures or to dear ones is to be abandoned. Then, when we try to avoid craving that person or thing, we face an internal civil war: our emotions say, "I want this," and our intellect says, "No! You're bad!" Such an internal battle is useless. Instead we can pause, examine our lives, and conclude that attachment makes us dissatisfied and unhappy. With such irrefutable proof of its disadvantages, we'll no longer want to get involved with it.

## HAPPINESS NOW AND IN THE FUTURE

Understanding the faults of attachment, we'll determine to be free from clinging to the happiness of this life and all the sufferings it brings. Of course, we'll still want to be happy now, but we won't be obsessed with getting everything we think we need or want. In addition, we'll recognize the importance of preparing for future lives.

The principal method to prepare for future lives and to eliminate turmoil in the present life is to observe cause and effect—karma—by abandoning destructive actions and practicing constructive ones.

To follow cause and effect, we must train ourselves in the techniques to subdue gross attachment, anger, jealousy, ignorance, deluded doubt and pride. Although the wisdom realizing emptiness is the ultimate way to subdue these disturbing emotions, for us beginners, meditation on impermanence is a good general antidote.

The meditation on impermanence involves recollecting that all the people, objects and situations change each moment. They don't stay the same. Remembering impermanence helps us to avoid exaggerating the importance of what happens to us. For example, if we're attached to our new car and are angry because someone dented it, we can think, "This car is always changing. It won't last forever. Since the day it was made, it's been deteriorating. I can enjoy it while it's here. But I don't need to be upset when it's dented, for the nature of the car is that it changes."

Some people, thinking this is a pessimistic view of life, say, "Everything changes, therefore there's nothing to live for." It's true that none of the people, possessions or situations we now have will last forever. That's the reality in which we live, and it can't be altered. However, impermanence also means new things can happen. Impermanence allows for a helpless baby to grow into a skilled adult. Impermanence means our love, compassion, wisdom and skills can increase.

Each disturbing emotion also has a particular antidote. For attachment, we can contemplate the undesirable aspects of the object in order to balance our overestimation of its good qualities. For anger, we can remember that others want to be happy and to avoid suffering just as we do. Because they are confused about how to do so, they harm other beings. As we understand others' situations and remember their kindness, we'll develop patience and love in response to their harm.

Rejoicing at others' happiness, good qualities and virtues is the remedy to jealousy. Studying and contemplating the Dharma cures ignorance. Breathing meditation frees us from the chatter and turbulence of deluded doubt. Pride is remedied by contemplating an extremely difficult subject, because then we'll see how little we know. Another remedy for pride is to remember that everything we know or have comes from others, and therefore there's no reason to be proud because we have it.

Calming these disturbing attitudes and developing detachment doesn't mean we give away all our money and live as beggars. We need money to function in society. There's nothing intrinsically good or bad about money. It's our attitude about it that's important, and thus we can develop a balanced view towards it. If we have a good income, very good; if we don't, we can still feel happy and successful. When we have money, we'll happily share it with others. We won't try to buy friends or brag about our resources, and as a result we won't be suspicious of others' motives. Because we won't be obsessed with having a certain income, we won't cheat others in business or deceive them in order to earn more. Others will trust us, and we won't feel ashamed of our actions.

Similarly, there is nothing intrinsically wrong with getting a good education or a good job. Whether these are beneficial or not depends on our motivation. If we study and train in a skill with the motivation to be able to offer service to others, our minds are peaceful and studying becomes a virtuous action. We can still want to do well on our exams and in our jobs—not because we want to have a good reputation or flaunt our wealth, but because we want to have a skill with which we can benefit others and improve our society.

Buddhism isn't opposed to material and technological progress. This can improve the lives of many people. However, Buddhism stresses the need for balancing material and spiritual concerns, because external progress alone doesn't make the world a happier place. Some modern societies have grave social problems and many unhappy people. If we develop nuclear energy but don't have a sense of morality to govern how we use it, it does more harm than good. If we live in wealthy, high-tech societies but are enslaved by our desires and anger, we can't enjoy what we have.

Therefore, Buddhism says external progress must be coupled with internal development. We need moral values, good ethics and a sense of responsibility for the welfare of everyone. In addition to loving-kindness and tolerance, we need wisdom. Then we can enjoy technological advancements while minimizing their unwanted side-effects.

It may seem paradoxical, but the less we're attached to the

finite pleasures of this life, the more we'll have a happy and peaceful life! Being unattached doesn't mean we "tune out" and don't enjoy life. It's quite the opposite, for with detachment we'll be more relaxed and less anxious. This naturally allows us to relate to our environment and to other people in a more caring way. As we stop frantically grasping at our current happiness, we'll become more able to enjoy everything around us.

## LET'S GET OFF THE FERRIS WHEEL

The first level of the determination to be free involves wanting to be free from unfortunate rebirths and the negative actions that cause these rebirths. However, does securing a good rebirth solve all of our problems? Will we find perfect and unending happiness in any rebirth we take?

When we examine what could happen to us in future lives, we discover that even if we're reborn as a human or as a celestial being with fantastic sensual pleasure, it doesn't last forever. We'll face problems in those lives too. Securing a good rebirth is thus a stopgap method to evade severe suffering. It helps for a while. But there isn't lasting happiness to be found in any rebirth in cyclic existence.

It's like riding on a ferris wheel that never stops: we go up and down continuously. As long as we're under the influence of ignorance and disturbing attitudes and actions, we aren't free. We're trapped in the ferris wheel and obliged to go 'round and 'round, taking one rebirth and then another, without choice.

Seeing this situation, we'll think, "There may seem to be many nice things to see on the ferris wheel, but it's actually boring." We'll realize there's nothing in any realm of existence that's worth being attached to. All the pleasures in cyclic existence are temporary, and they don't compensate for the fact that we continuously undergo birth and death.

Thinking in this way brings us to the second level of the determination to be free. We'll feel, "It's fine to get good rebirths, but as long as I'm born anywhere in cyclic existence, I'm going to experience problems and difficulties without choice. This is a totally unsatisfactory situation. I want to be free from it!''

We wish for a state of lasting peace and happiness free from all undesirable circumstances. Seeing that all difficulties of cyclic existence are caused by ignorance, disturbing attitudes, and actions done under their influence, we'll seek a method to free ourselves from these and to abide in nirvana, a state of liberation and happiness. Thus, the great Tibetan sage Lama Tzong Khapa said in *The Foundation of All Good Qualities*:

> There is no satisfaction in enjoying worldly pleasures.
> They are the door to all misery. Having realized that
> the fault of the pleasures of cyclic existence is that they
> cannot be trusted, may I be strongly intent on the bliss
> of liberation—inspire me thus!

The method to completely eradicate disturbing attitudes and actions is to develop the three higher trainings: ethical conduct, concentration and wisdom. With ethical conduct, we'll avoid destructive actions. On this foundation, we'll practice concentration to subdue the gross disturbing attitudes and gain the ability to direct our minds to whatever object of meditation we wish, for as long as we wish. By combining concentration with wisdom, we'll penetrate the meaning of reality and thus eliminate our ignorance, disturbing attitudes and the karmic imprints that produce suffering.

Let's now look at ethical conduct, as it's the foundation for all higher practices.

# 3 Ethics:
## Relating to others constructively

Having understood our great potential, we become interested
in what we can do to develop it. Which actions are beneficial?
Which actions obscure our human beauty and interfere with
our spiritual progress, and thus should be abandoned? The
answers lie in the subject of ethics.

The Buddhist view on ethics is derived from the link between our actions and their effects. Actions are termed "negative" because they bring unpleasant results and "positive" because they result in happiness for both ourselves and others.
Because we want happiness and we don't want suffering, it's
wise to learn about and to live according to the functioning
of cause and effect. Understanding the results which certain
actions bring, we are then better able to decide how we wish
to act.

As a guideline, the Buddha advised us to avoid ten actions
because they destroy the happiness of ourselves and others.
Three are physical: killing, stealing and unwise sexual behavior.
Four are verbal: lying, slander, harsh words and idle talk. Three
are mental: coveting others' possessions, maliciousness and
wrong views.

## THREE PHYSICAL ACTIONS

Killing refers to taking the life of any living being. This is the most serious of the ten destructive actions, because it's the most harmful to others. All beings, humans and animals alike, cherish their lives above all else. We may sometimes be presented with difficult situations in which it may seem advantageous to kill: our country is attacked, a person or animal threatens to harm our child, our house is infested with termites. If we think creatively, there are often other solutions besides taking another's life: diplomacy rather than weapons can stop an aggressor, while trapping a threatening animal or knocking it unconscious stops the danger. As much as possible, we should avoid taking others' lives.

Euthanasia and abortion are difficult issues. From a Buddhist perspective, they both involve taking life. Nevertheless, a clear-cut answer in a specific situation is rarely available. Such situations challenge our intelligence and our compassion. We must think deeply about the advantages and disadvantages to ourselves and others of all the alternatives, and do what we feel is best.

Stealing is taking what isn't given. This ranges from armed robbery to borrowing something from a friend and not returning it. Avoiding paying taxes or fees we should pay is another form of stealing, as is taking things from our workplace for our personal use.

With a wish to avoid misusing others' property, we'll become more mindful of our attitude and actions towards others' possessions. This is very useful and helps to prevent much conflict with those around us. In addition, others will trust us and be willing to loan us things. They also won't be fearful that their things will disappear when we're around.

Unwise sexual behavior chiefly refers to adultery: we're involved in a relationship—whether we're married or not—and have intercourse with someone else. If we're single but our partner is involved with someone else, this is also unwise sexual behavior. Sexual activity that spreads disease or otherwise harms ourselves or others should be avoided.

## FOUR VERBAL ACTIONS

Lying is deliberately saying what we know isn't true. Although lying is chiefly a verbal action, it also can be done physically, through a nod or gesture. Not only does lying bring us harm in future lives, it also destroys our present relationships. If we lie, others won't trust us even when we do tell the truth.

Sometimes we encounter delicate situations when telling the truth would hurt someone's feelings. For example, our friends invite us for dinner and ask how we're enjoying the meal. We think the food isn't very good, but it would hurt them if we said this. However, if we answer by saying, "I really appreciate your care and concern in asking me over for supper. This food is cooked with love," we're both expressing our gratitude truthfully and avoiding lying about the taste of the food.

If an angry person with a gun asks us, "Where is Pat?" we would endanger Pat's life by responding truthfully. Rather, we can avoid the question or give an irrelevant answer. As in all cases involving these ten destructive actions, we have to use our common sense!

Slandering others is frequently done out of jealousy. For example, we wish to get a promotion, so we criticize our colleagues to the boss. Or, if our good friend is now friends with someone else, we may want to break up their relationship. So, we tell each one about bad things the other has said. Words that cause disharmony in others' relationships or prevent those who are already not getting along from reconciling are considered slander.

The disadvantages of divisive words are apparent. Others will soon discover what we're up to and will cease being friendly. We'll have the reputation of being a "trouble-maker," and others will avoid us.

Harsh words include obvious actions such as shouting with anger, maliciously criticizing others and making fun of them. It also includes teasing if we're seeking to hurt another or making someone else look foolish. Sometimes harsh words can be said with a smile, such as when we "innocently" say something we know another is sensitive about.

Although part of us may feel we're justified in using harsh words, if we look deeper, are we happy with ourselves when we do? Although we may out-shout someone and barrage them until we win the argument, do we feel good about ourselves later? What kind of person are we if we're happy when we embarrass someone or make him/her look stupid or inept? If we closely examine how we speak to others, we'll discover why others sometimes don't want to be in our company. However, if we develop respect for others and concern about their feelings, not only are we developing self-respect, but also others will be drawn towards us.

Idle talk is one of the principal ways in which we waste our time and create disturbances in others' minds. Although we may lack time to attend a Dharma talk or to visit an irritable relative who is sick, we hardly ever lack time to talk about movie stars, sports, what the neighbors are doing, the latest cars and fashions. In the evening we're too tired to meditate or to pay serious attention to what our child or spouse confides in us, but we can stay up late chatting about this and that.

Sometimes the more we talk about a problem, the more solid it becomes. What started out as a small difficulty becomes big in our minds after our friend has vouched for our position and assured us the other person is wrong. Then, when our friend tells someone else who in turn tells others, the small problem becomes enormous.

This isn't to say we shouldn't discuss our problems or confide in others. Many times it's helpful to get another person's view on a situation. But when we seek our friend's "advice" merely to validate our own position rather than to explore compassionate solutions to the problem, then the conversation has deteriorated into idle talk.

Nor is this to say that joking, laughing and having a good time are "bad." Not at all! Discouraging idle talk is a call to develop good motivations for talking with people. If we laugh and chat only for our own amusement, we're not using our life to its fullest. On the other hand, with concern for someone who is depressed, we can try to lift his or her spirits by laughing and talking about this and that. Sometimes we need to relax so we can engage in serious work again. At this time, we can chat with friends, still being conscientious not to disturb anyone's mind with what we say.

## THREE MENTAL ACTIONS

No one necessarily knows when we commit any of the three destructive mental actions. Nevertheless, they leave negative tendencies on our mindstreams. Coveting others' possessions occurs when we notice someone's desirable possession, and plan how to get it. We may think, "I'll drop a hint about how nice this is and maybe she'll give it to me. Or, I could flatter her and she'll want to give me a gift." Coveting makes us restless and may lead us to act or speak destructively. We would be happier if we trained ourselves to be content with our possessions and to rejoice at others' fortune.

Maliciousness is cultivating ill will and the thought to harm another. We're quite good at this. We may devise an intricate plan to revenge a wrong done to us, or we consider what to say to hurt someone and "put him in his place." Sometimes we're not even aware that our minds are engaged in malicious thoughts. We need to observe our thoughts carefully to know when we're wishing others harm or rejoicing at their misfortune.

Having wrong views is denying the existence of something that exists or asserting the existence of that which is non-existent. This applies to important topics that mold our entire outlook on life. For example, if we firmly think, "There is no rebirth," and closed-mindedly refuse to listen to others' opinions, then we have fallen into wrong views. Our present doubt about rebirth isn't a wrong view, for we're exploring new ideas and are open to others' arguments. Wrong views occur when someone emphatically and antagonistically holds an erroneous philosophical or ethical view.

When we refrain from engaging in the ten destructive actions, we're automatically practicing the ten constructive ones. As we become more aware of our behavior, our lives and the lives of the people around us will become much more peaceful. The world's religions share a similar view of ethical conduct which revolves around abandoning these ten destructive actions.

It takes time to change our behavior. First we must learn to recognize the specific destructive action we do. Often, we aren't aware of what we think, say and do, because we're busy, distracted, proud or careless. Sometimes we don't recognize until years later that we hurt someone.

After recognizing the destructive actions, effort is needed to refrain from doing them again. This is harder than it seems, for if we habitually act in a certain way, will-power alone isn't sufficient to change our behavior. We must deeply understand the disadvantages of this behavior and repeatedly be attentive and try to avoid it. Many techniques for changing our destructive attitudes are found in Buddhist teachings. It's useful to study and practice these in daily life. At first we may not be very successful, but with consistent yet gentle effort, we can change. In this process of self-cultivation, it's important to be patient with ourselves.

Some people want to attain spiritual realizations, but they don't want to change their daily actions. They lie and cheat others when it's convenient, they gossip about irrelevant subjects and criticize the people they don't like. Yet, they want to do advanced meditational practices and gain extraordinary powers.

In fact, they aren't creating the causes to have realizations. If we can't control our grossest actions—what we do and say to others—how can we expect to change our minds, which are the source of all of our actions? It's much easier to control what we say and do than to control our negative emotions and attitudes. Thus we start by eliminating the three physical negative actions and the four verbal ones. Simultaneously we'll put effort into avoiding the three destructive mental actions. With this as a foundation, we'll be prepared to engage in more advanced practices. The Buddha said:

> Benevolent and ethical,
> With the positive potential from what they do,
> The wise always find happiness
> Here and in the beyond.

# 4 Nurturing Altruism:
## The open heart of love and compassion

The second principal realization of the path is the altruistic intention to attain enlightenment in order to benefit all beings. In Sanskrit it is called "bodhicitta," which has several English translations: awakening mind, bodhi mind, dedicated heart and thought of enlightenment. People who have this motivation—bodhisattvas—have such unselfish, impartial and intense love and compassion for others that they seek to attain enlightenment in order to be most capable of benefiting them.

We live in a universe full of other beings. Despite the fact that we have different bodies and different experiences, we're very similar. All of us have problems and disturbing attitudes. We're all reborn and die again and again. Each of us has the same deeply-rooted wish only to have happiness and to avoid all difficulties.

Realizing we're all in the same boat, how could we possibly justify working only for our own benefit? Others' pain and problems make them as unhappy as our pain and problems make us. How can we say we're more important than other people? What logic or rationale is there to our constant cherishing of ourselves more than others?

If we think democratically we see that there's one of me while there's an infinite number of other beings. If we compare the happiness of one person to the happiness of all beings, it no longer seems fair to be concerned only with our own welfare. We can't follow a spiritual path seeking only our own happiness. We've got to help others find happiness too.

It's difficult to help all others when our own minds are partial. We tend to like some people more than others and go out of our way to help them. We're unkind to people we consider obnoxious and don't like. As long as we perceive and categorize others as friends, enemies or strangers, and respectively generate attachment, aversion or apathetic indifference towards them, it will be difficult for us to help them. First we need to have impartial love and compassion for all of them.

The foundation of love is realizing that others aren't inherently our friends, enemies or strangers. A friend can become a stranger or an enemy. Someone we don't like can become a friend or a stranger. A stranger can become a friend or an enemy. These relationships change according to time and circumstances. If we look in our own lives, we'll find many examples of this. Because our relationships with others are changing, it makes no sense to put others into hard and fast categories and to have strong feelings of attachment, aversion or indifference towards them.

If we had a larger perspective we would see how arbitrary it is to label people as friends, enemies and strangers. Someone gives us a thousand dollars today and becomes our friend. Tomorrow he slaps us and thus becomes our enemy. Another person slaps us today and gives us a thousand dollars tomorrow. Which one is the friend and which is the enemy?

Friend and enemy are arbitrary distinctions, depending on time and circumstances, and on our labeling a person "friend" or "enemy." If we could remember the relationships we've had with all beings—including those in previous lives—we would see that all of them have at different times been our friend, our enemy and a stranger.

Generally, we consider someone who is kind to us and agrees

with our opinions as a good person and real friend. We think of someone we don't get along with as a bad person and a real enemy. But both people have good and bad qualities. We're just seeing a few of each person's qualities, emphasizing them and thinking that's the person's character.

Our view of others is very subjective. When we look at a certain person she appears wonderful, while to another person she appears obnoxious. Why? This occurs because we're looking at her from one point of view, while the other person is regarding her from another. Actually, she has both good qualities and weaknesses.

If we train ourselves to have a more complete view of others, then we'll cease to be disappointed when our dear ones don't conform to our expectations. We'll recognize and accept their weaknesses. Also, our intolerance and disrespect for people we previously judged as unlikeable will decrease because we'll be aware of their good qualities. Although their kindness may not be directed towards us at this moment, they are kind to many others.

When we consider all aspects of others' personalities and are aware of the changeable and subjective nature of relationships, we'll be much more balanced in our feelings for others. Without the thorns of attachment, aversion and apathetic indifference, our hearts will open more to others.

## THE KINDNESS OF OTHERS

On the basis of equanimity for all beings, we can then cultivate love and compassion. The first step in generating love and compassion is to remember the kindness of others.

Everything we have depends on the kindness of others. Our food is grown, transported and often cooked by others. Our clothes are made by others. Our home depends on the kind efforts of many others: architects, engineers, construction workers, plumbers, electricians, painters, carpenters. If we look closely, everything we enjoy comes from the labor of others.

Some people say, "But sometimes these people don't do their

work well. They are irresponsible and pollute the environment. Even if they do their job well, they're working for money, not because they want to help us."

These points are well-taken. But it's very curious how, on one hand, we want to regard others as kind and have warm feelings towards them, yet whenever we start to consider what they've done for us, another part of our minds recoils and says, "Yes, but...," and then lists others' faults.

Still, to reply to the above doubts: yes, some people make mistakes and do harmful actions either intentionally or unintentionally. But they're doing the best they can, given their mental and physical circumstances. If people are harming others or making serious mistakes, we should try to remedy the situation. However, we can do that without being angry at them.

One of my teachers, Lama Yeshe, used to tell us, "They mean well, dear." Even people who harm others or who work recklessly are just trying to be happy. Given their own ignorance and confusion, they're doing what they think is right.

People may work for money, without intending to be kind to us. But, the point isn't why they work, it's that we benefit from their efforts. Regardless of whether they are working for money or reputation, the fact is that if they didn't do their job, we would be worse off.

Someone may say, "I pay people for their work, so they're only doing what they're employed to do. How is that kindness?" Even when we pay people to do a job, we still benefit from their efforts. In addition, the money that we pay them isn't *ours*. We weren't born with handfuls of money! The money we have came because others gave it to us. If it weren't for the kindness of our employer or our customers, how would we have money?

When we were born we had nothing. We couldn't even feed ourselves or protect ourselves from cold or heat. It is solely due to the kindness of our parents that we didn't die when we were infants.

We may feel we're intelligent and knowledgeable, but where

did these qualities come from? Our parents taught us to speak, and our teachers instructed us in many skills and subjects. Although as children we may not have appreciated what our parents and teachers did for us, if we now look back at it, we'll see that they helped us greatly.

Some people have been abused as children or have experienced horrible situations as refugees or war victims. How can they begin to consider others as kind when the harm they received was so devastating?

First, we can think deeply about the people who have been kind to us. Whether it's from a refugee worker, a teacher, a companion or a stranger whose smile conveyed understanding and care, all of us have received kindness. It's helpful to recall even small instances of others' kindness, for that softens our hurt and opens our heart to return affection.

Then we can examine whether or not the person or people who have harmed us did so perpetually. Perhaps we had some neutral experiences or even some positive ones with them. Remembering these helps us to see that those who have harmed us aren't thoroughly corrupt personalities.

In addition we can think that those who harmed us acted out of their own confusion and ignorance. Although they simply wanted to be happy, they employed the wrong means and harmed both themselves and others. Thinking in this way we can slowly begin to forgive them and to heal our emotional wounds.

## OPEN HEART

Buddhists believe that the kindness of others becomes even more apparent when we consider that we have had many lives. In each of our lives, others have been kind to us. We haven't always been with the people we're close to now. In past lives we have had every kind of relationship with every other being. We've been each other's parents and children many times in the past, even though we can't remember it now.

This may seem strange at first, but when we consider the

significance of beginningless lives, we can understand that we've known everyone else before. In those previous lives when others were our parents, they were generally very kind to us. Even when they weren't our parents, they helped us.

When we consider this deeply, we'll feel overwhelming appreciation and gratitude towards others. Then, when we think of others, they'll appear inexpressibly kind in our eyes. We'll sincerely want to repay their kindness. From our hearts, we'll want them to be happy. This is love.

This open heart of love makes us feel joyful. But how do we feel when we're selfish? Our hearts are fearful, tight and uncomfortable. Does selfishness help? Our self-cherishing attitude pretends to care for us by saying, "If I don't take care of myself first, who will? In this world, I've got to look out for my own welfare before anyone else's."

In actual fact, this attitude destroys us. If we examine our experiences, we'll notice that every time we're in agitated conflict with others, selfishness is involved. Every time we act destructively, thus creating the cause for our own future misery, the self-cherishing mind is behind it. Whenever we are lazy, demanding or ungrateful, we are under the influence of the selfish attitude. Why do countries go to war? Why are there conflicts in families? Why do some people abuse drugs and alcohol, power and wealth? The answer always comes down to selfishness, caring more for oneself than for others.

A very effective technique to lessen the selfish attitude when it arises is to imagine ourselves surrounded by many people. This reminds us that we share the world with others. Then, instead of identifying with ourselves, we identify with the others and look back at our old selves. How do we appear in the eyes of others? Are we as important as we previously thought?

In fact, there are many others and only one "me." Therefore, is it fair to be concerned with my welfare alone? Is it correct to consider my happiness to be more important than that of others? Thinking this way helps us to put the situation in an accurate perspective.

This isn't to say we're bad people because we're sometimes

selfish. The self-cherishing attitude is one of clouds obscuring the clear sky of our minds. We shouldn't mistakenly identify ourselves with the selfishness, for if we do, we only compound insult with injury. Here, we're determining to counteract selfishness because it harms ourselves and others.

On the other hand, great benefit comes from cherishing others. They'll be happy and we'll be happy. In addition, with care and concern for others, we'll act constructively. This brings the by-product of our own happiness in future lives. Our relationships will be more harmonious, and so will our environment. By cherishing others more than ourselves, our minds will become noble and we'll progress along the path to enlightenment. The great Indian sage Shantideva said:

> Whatever joy there is in this world
> All comes from desiring others to be happy,
> And whatever suffering there is in this world
> All comes from (selfishly) desiring ourselves to be
>       happy.
>
> But what need is there to say much more?
> The childish work for their own benefit,
> The Buddhas work for the benefit of others.
> Just look at the difference between them!

## LOVE AND COMPASSION

Love is the wish for others to be happy, while compassion is the wish for them to be free from all suffering. Love and compassion can be impartial and extend to everyone when we have eliminated attachment to friends, anger towards enemies and indifference to strangers. Love isn't a limited commodity that has to be parceled out sparingly. When we recognize others' kindness and respect their wish to be happy and to avoid problems, our love can become limitless.

Some people may wonder, "Isn't this a bit impractical? Am I supposed to give up my family? Or do I love everyone equally and have many wives or husbands?! Do I let thieves into my house and show them where the money is because I love them?"

Love must be combined with wisdom. It's not stupid love. Towards our family we can cultivate love rather than attachment. We may have equal love for all beings, but still live with our family.

Love and sexual desire are different. Our equal affection for everyone doesn't need to be expressed sexually. Similarly, encouraging criminal activity such as burglary isn't love. However, we may use our resources to help others get a good education and a job so they needn't resort to burglary.

Love is an internal attitude of care and concern for all. Nevertheless, we have to act appropriately in each situation, doing what is most beneficial for the greatest number of people. If we have to stop someone who is harming others, we can do so not out of anger or revenge, but out of concern for the perpetrator as well as for the others in the situation. Mentally and emotionally our reaction to all beings will be equal. However, verbally and physically we'll still act appropriately in each situation.

In addition to love, we can develop compassion, wishing others to be free from their problems and the causes of their unsatisfactory situations. This compassion extends equally to everyone, no matter who they are or how they act.

Compassion is different from pity. Pity is a proud, condescending attitude: "I'm such a good person helping those poor, unfortunate people whose lives are falling apart." Compassion, on the other hand, regards others as equal to ourselves, for all of us equally want happiness and don't want problems. With respect and humility, seeking no recognition for our actions, we'll then help in whatever way we're able. We'll help others with the same ease and lack of expectation as when we help ourselves.

With love and compassion we'll go on to develop the great resolve to take upon ourselves the responsibility for the happiness of others. Without this great resolve, even if we have love and compassion, we may not be motivated to act. Like a person who watches someone else drowning, thinking "Oh, this is dreadful. This person has got to be saved," we may never have the thought to actually jump in and help. Having fully developed the great resolve, however, we will automatically do whatever we can for others, without hesitating or feeling obliged or inconvenienced. The great resolve converts the feelings of love and compassion into action.

How can we most effectively work for the welfare of others? Although we may wish to help others, at the present our own abilities are limited. Our compassion is incomplete, we're short of wisdom, our skillful means are poor. Who has these qualities which are necessary to benefit others in the best way?

When we look around, we see worldly beings are short of these qualities. The holy beings—the arhats and bodhisattvas—have developed them to a great extent, but not fully. Only the Buddhas have perfectly eliminated all obscurations from their mindstreams and completely developed all qualities. Seeing this, we too will aspire to become a Buddha in order to benefit all beings. This is the altruistic intention, the second principal realization of the path.

When we have this altruistic intention spontaneously day and night, we'll be called bodhisattvas. The next step will be to perfect the six far-reaching attitudes (the six *paramitas*): generosity, ethical conduct, patience, joyous effort, meditative stabilization and wisdom. This is the path to the full enlightenment of a Buddha. Two of the most important factors in attaining enlightenment, wisdom and meditation, will be explored next.

# 5 *Wisdom Realizing Reality:*
## Cutting the root of ignorance

Having developed the determination to be free and the altruistic intention to attain enlightenment in order to benefit others, how do we actualize these aspirations? To be free from our difficulties in the cycle of constantly recurring problems, the Buddha said we must eradicate their root cause: the ignorance that grasps at a truly-existent, independently-existent self. This is done by gaining wisdom, which is the third principal realization of the path. Lama Tzong Khapa in *The Three Principles of the Path* emphasized the importance of wisdom:

> Even if you meditate upon the determination to be free and the altruistic intention, without the wisdom realizing the final nature (emptiness of inherent existence), you cannot cut the root of cyclic existence. Therefore, strive for the means to realize dependent arising.

To cleanse our mindstreams totally from all obscurations and develop our potential to become a Buddha we must eliminate the subtle stains of ignorance. This too is done by generating the wisdom realizing emptiness. In short, the realization of emptiness is not only the most effective purification practice, but also the key to knowing reality and to discriminating what exists from what does not.

The subject of emptiness is difficult to understand. To have a full understanding takes time, dedicated study and meditation. What is presented below is only a taste. It's not meant to be a pat explanation, and it'll probably generate doubts and questions in your mind. This is okay, for in Buddhism we're not expected to understand and accept everything instantly.

Realizing emptiness doesn't mean making our minds blank, without any thoughts. Some animals don't think very much, and there's nothing virtuous about that. The emptiness that we seek to realize also isn't like the emptiness of our stomachs when we're hungry. Instead, the emptiness perceived by this wisdom is the lack of all fantasized ways of existing that we've projected onto people and phenomena. It's a lack, or absence, of a false way of existing.

First, we have to understand what it is that we're negating. What is it that people and phenomena are empty of? They lack being independently, truly or inherently existent. Unfortunately, from beginningless time, we've been so accustomed to the seeming appearance of independently existent phenomena and have been so used to grasping at this appearance as correct, that we fail to detect that it is false. We aren't aware that people and phenomena do not exist in the way they appear to.

## LOOKING FOR THE REAL CRACKER

How do things appear to exist to us? Let's take a cracker, for example. It appears to us to be a real cracker. Anyone who walks in this room should be able to identify this as a cracker because there's some "crackerness" to it. There is something about it or in it that makes it a cracker and not anything else. It is *one* solid cracker, which exists "out there," independent of our minds. It was there—a cracker in its own right—and we just happened to come along and see it. This cracker is findable: it's right there!

The cracker appears to us to exist "out there," independent

of causes and conditions, independent of parts, and independent of our minds and the concepts and labels we apply to it. But if the cracker really existed in this way, then when we analyze and search for this real cracker, we should definitely be able to find it.

We're looking for the real, independent cracker that appears to us to exist ''out there.'' We're searching for the thing that is the cracker. If we break the cracker in half, is the real cracker in one half or in the other half? Or is it in both? If we say the cracker is in both, then we must have two crackers since we have two separate pieces. That certainly is an easy way to make crackers!

If we say the cracker is in one half rather than in the other, why is one piece the cracker while the other piece isn't? Even if we do accept the bigger piece as being the cracker, then what about it or in it is the cracker? We should be able to find the cracker and the ''crackerness'' quality somewhere in it. But if we continue to break it into pieces in an attempt to find the real cracker, we'll end up with a mess, not a cracker! We'll have a pile of crumbs, and what about that is a cracker?

The real, independent cracker that appeared to exist is unfindable when we analyze and attempt to locate it.

If there were some inherent cracker there, we should have been able to find it either among its parts or separate from its parts. But, it isn't its parts, and it isn't anywhere else either. If the cracker were separate from its parts, then the toasted combination of flour and water could be on this plate and the cracker could be across the room. That's hardly the case, for apart from the toasted dough, what else could be called ''cracker''?

Nor is the cracker the collection of its parts, for a collection is just a group of parts. If none of the parts by itself is a cracker, how can many parts together be an independent cracker with some quality of cracker-ness? Just as a collection of non-butterflies, for example grasshoppers, doesn't make a butterfly, a group of non-crackers—that is, a group of crumbs—can't suddenly make a real cracker that exists as a cracker from its own side.

This leads us to conclude that there was no inherent cracker to start with. In other words, the real, solid and findable cracker that appeared to us and that we grasped as existing independently, doesn't exist. That's not to say there's no cracker there at all, only that the independent cracker doesn't exist. That cracker doesn't exist in the way it appeared to. It doesn't exist in the way we thought it did.

However, the cracker still exists. If it didn't, we couldn't eat it! Although it doesn't exist in an independent fashion, it does exist dependently. It depends on its causes and conditions: the flour, water, baker and so on. It depends on its parts: the various sections that compose it, as well as its color and shape, its smell, taste, and so on. And, it also depends on our conventionally conceiving of it and labeling it "cracker." As a society, we've agreed to consider this accumulation of parts that serves a particular function as a unique phenomenon, and give it the name "cracker" to distinguish it from other things.

We searched for something that is a cracker from its own side, independent of its parts, independent of our minds with their concepts and labels. That independent, real cracker can't be found, because it doesn't exist. But, a dependently existent cracker is there. That's what we're eating.

How does the cracker exist? A group of atoms are put together in a certain pattern. Our minds look at that, conceive it to be one thing, and give it the name "cracker." It becomes a cracker because all of us have conceived of it in a similar way and have agreed, by the force of social convention, to give it the name "cracker." In the *Questions of Upali Sutra*, it says:

> These alluring blossoming flowers of various colors
> And these fascinating brilliant mansions of gold
> Are without any (inherently existent) maker here.
> They are posited through the power of conceptuality.
> The world is imputed through the power of
>     conceptuality.

That cracker exists dependently. Apart from this dependently existent cracker, there is no other cracker. It's empty of being a cracker inherently, independently, with some cracker-ness nature to it. The cracker exists, but it doesn't exist in the same way it appears to exist. It appears to be independent, when in fact it isn't. It depends upon its causes and conditions, parts and our minds which conceive it to be a "cracker." The cracker is a dependently arising phenomenon.

## WHO ARE WE?

If there is no essential, independent cracker, is there an independent me? Is there a real "I," a findable person?

The Buddha's answer differs from the Judeo-Christian idea of an eternal, unchanging soul and from the Hindu notion of "atman." We should be able to find the soul, atman or inherent self, something that is the person, when we analyze and search for it. Can we?

Remember a situation in which you were extremely angry. How does the "I" appear to exist at that moment? It seems very solid. There is a real me that someone is insulting. That "I" has to be defended. The "I," the self, feels findable; it is somewhere inside our body-mind complex.

If that solid, true, independent "I" exists as it appears to us, we should be able to find it, either in our body and mind or separate from them. There is no other place "I" could be.

Am I my body? If I am, then which part of my body is me? My arm? My stomach? My brain? All of my organs are composed of atoms. They aren't me. Nor is my entire body me, for if it were, then after I die, my corpse would be me. I am something more than the atoms that compose the body, for physical matter alone, without consciousness, can't perceive objects, and I am cognizant.

Am I my mind? If so, then am I my eye consciousness, which perceives color and shape? My ear consciousness, which perceives sound? My mental consciousness, the one that thinks? Am I a particular personality characteristic? If I were my anger, then I should always be angry. If I were my intelligence, then I should always be intelligent.

Nor am I a collection of all these various mental qualities and states of mind, because a collection of things, each of which isn't a real and independent me, can't become me.

Although it may feel that there is some "thinker" or some internal thing that makes our decisions, when we search for that one particular thing, we can't find it. Decisions and thoughts arise depending upon many mental factors. There is no little guy in there running the show.

The collection of my body and mind isn't an independent self, for it's a collection of parts. It is dependent on those parts. How could a real independent me be found in the collection of my body and mind, neither of which is me?

Nor do I exist as something separate from the body and mind. If I did, then I should be able to identify and find my self where there was neither my body nor my mind. That would mean that I could be in one place, while my body and mind were in another! That's clearly impossible. The self, or I, is linked and related to the body and mind.

Are we some independent entity that goes from one lifetime to the next? At the time of death, our minds absorb into more and more subtle states. The subtlest level of mind goes from one life to the next. However, this extremely subtle mind is constantly changing each moment. It never remains the same in two consecutive instants, just as on a physical level the arrangement of electrons in an atom changes in each instant. We can't point to one moment of our mind which has been and always will be us. We aren't yesterday's mind, we aren't today's mind or tomorrow's mind. We aren't the mind that leaves this body at death, nor are we the mind that is reborn. What we call "I" is dependent upon all of these, but it isn't any one of them.

Remembering the example of a river can help us to understand this. The Mississippi River isn't it's banks. It's not the water or the rocks or the streams that feed into it. A real, independent river appears to exist when we aren't analyzing, but as soon as we question, "What is this independent river that

appears to exist?'' we can't find anything to point to. Yet, there
is a dependently existing river.

Similarly, our mindstream isn't any particular moment of
mind, nor is it the collection of moments. Such a truly-existent
mindstream doesn't exist. Our mind is empty of true or inherent existence. Still, there is the continuum of moments of
mind that form the mindstream, and this takes rebirth.

The "I" or the self doesn't exist independently of the body
and mind. Nor can it be found within the body or mind. Nor
is it the body and mind together. In other words, the solid,
truly existing "I" we felt when we were angry can't be found
anywhere. Why not? Because it doesn't exist. The "I" is empty
of being independently existent. This is what is meant by selflessness or emptiness.

## DEPENDENT EXISTENCE

That doesn't mean the "I" doesn't exist at all. What we are
negating is its independent or inherent existence. We do exist. If we were completely non-existent, then who is writing
this book and who is reading it?

We dependently exist. We depend on causes: the sperm and
egg of our parents, our consciousness that came from another
life. We depend on parts: our body and mind. We depend on
concept and label as well: on the basis of our body and mind
being together, we conceive of this as a person and give it the
label "I." We exist by being merely labeled on a suitable basis, our body and mind. The Buddha said in the sutras:

> Just as a chariot is designated
> In dependence upon collections of parts,
> So, conventionally, a sentient being
> (Is designated) in dependence upon the aggregates
>     (body and mind).

It's important to understand that realizing emptiness doesn't
destroy the "I." An independent, solid, real "I" never existed. What we are destroying is the ignorance which holds

on to the idea that such a solid "I" exists.

It's not the case that there used to be real things, and as soon as we meditate on emptiness, we destroy them. It's not that things used to be independently existent, and then we take this quality away from them. We simply realize independent existence was never there, and thus we eliminate the misconception that independently existing things exist.

There is a person who attains enlightenment. This is the conventional I, which depends on causes and conditions, parts, and on concept and label. Enlightened beings don't have the strong sense of a separate and solid "I" that we do, for they have realized that such an I doesn't exist. The self still exists, but in a gentler and softer way. It's merely a convention, not a real entity.

When we understand emptiness or selflessness properly, we have an extremely strong tool to subdue our disturbing attitudes. When we realize emptiness, we see there's no solid person who is angry; there's no real person whose reputation needs to be defended; there's no independently beautiful person or object that we have to possess. By realizing emptiness, our attachment, anger, jealousy, pride and ignorance vanish, because there's no real person who has to be protected, and there's no real object to be grasped.

This importance of realizing emptiness was stressed in the *The Superior Sutra of the King of Meditative Stabilization*:

> If the selflessness of phenomena is analyzed
> And if this analysis is cultivated in meditation,
> It causes the effect of attaining nirvana.
> Through no other cause does one come to peace.

Realizing emptiness doesn't mean we become inert and unambitious. If we think, "There's no real me, no real money. So why do anything?" then we don't have the correct understanding of emptiness. Realizing selflessness will give us tremendous space for action. Rather than our energy being consumed by attachment, anger and ignorance, we'll be free to use our wisdom and compassion in innumerable ways to benefit others.

Having generated the determination to be free from all un-satisfactory situations and the altruistic intention to attain en-lightenment, when we then meditate on emptiness, we can completely purify our minds of every defilement. Removing our limitations, we'll be able to develop our good qualities to perfection, so that we'll have all skillful means necessary to help others in the most effective ways. Our minds are capable of being transformed in this way. It's possible for us to go from confusion to enlightenment, from being an ordinary being to being a Buddha, by developing the three principal realizations of the path.

It takes time, patience and joyous effort to develop the three principal realizations. We also need concentration, so that when we meditate on these three topics our insights will be stable and penetrating.

# 6 *Meditation:*
## Developing concentration and insight

In Tibetan, the word "meditation" comes from the same verbal root as "to habituate" or "to familiarize." Thus, in meditation we endeavor to habituate ourselves to valuable ways of viewing the world. We also seek to familiarize ourselves with an accurate view of reality, so that we can eliminate all wrong conceptions and disturbing attitudes.

Meditation isn't merely chasing all thoughts out of our minds and abiding in a blank state. There's nothing spectacular about a blank mind. Skillfully directed thoughts can help us, especially at the initial levels of meditation. Eventually we need to transcend the limitations of concepts. However, doing so doesn't mean entering a lethargic blank state. It means clearly and directly perceiving reality.

First, we must listen to instructions on how to meditate and what to meditate on. Meditation isn't just sitting with crossed legs and closed eyes. It's directing our minds to a positive object and cultivating beneficial attitudes. We need to listen to instructions from an experienced teacher in order to know how to do this properly.

Second, we think about the instructions: we must understand a subject before we can habituate ourselves to it. This reflection can be done by discussing the teachings with our Dharma friends and teachers. It can also be done alone, seated in meditation position.

When we have some intellectual understanding of the subject, then we integrate it into our minds through meditation. Through familiarizing our minds with certain attitudes and views—such as impartial love or the wisdom realizing reality—they gradually become spontaneous in us.

There is a classic meditation position: we sit cross-legged on a cushion, with the backside higher than the legs. The shoulders are level and the back is straight, as if we were being pulled up from the crown of the head. The hands are placed in the lap, just below the navel. The right hand is on top of the left, with the thumbs touching. The arms are neither pressed against the body nor sticking out, but in a comfortable position. The head is slightly inclined, the mouth closed, with the tongue against the upper palate.

The eyes are slightly open in order to prevent drowsiness, but they aren't looking at anything. Rather, they're gazing downward, loosely focused at the tip of the nose or on the ground in front. Meditation is done entirely with the mental consciousness, not with the visual consciousness. We shouldn't try to "see" anything with our eyes during meditation.

It's good to meditate in the morning before beginning the day's activities as the mind is fresher then. By focusing on beneficial attitudes in our morning meditation, we'll be more alert and calmer during the day. Meditation in the evening also helps to settle the mind, and "digest" what happened during the day before going to sleep.

Meditation sessions shouldn't be too long at first. Choose a time that's reasonable for your capacity and your schedule. It's important to be regular in meditation practice because regular repetition is necessary to familiarize ourselves with beneficial attitudes. Meditating fifteen minutes every day is more beneficial than meditating three hours one day and then sleeping in the rest of the week.

Because our motivation determines whether what we do is

beneficial or not, it's extremely important to cultivate a good motivation before meditating. If we begin each meditation session with a strong motivation, it'll be easier to concentrate. Thus, for a few minutes prior to putting our attention on the object of meditation, we should think of the benefits of meditation for ourselves and others.

It's very worthwhile to generate the altruistic intention thus: "How wonderful it would be if all beings had happiness and were free of all difficulties! I would like to make this possible by showing others the path to enlightenment. But, as long as my own mind is unclear, I can't help myself let alone others. Therefore, I want to improve myself—to eliminate my obscurations and develop my potentials—so that I can be of better service to all others. For this reason, I'm going to do this meditation session, which will be one step more along the path."

Within Buddhism, there are many meditations. Basically, they're divided into two categories: those to gain samatha or calm abiding, and those to develop vipassana or special insight. The Buddha said in the sutra *Revealing the Thought of Buddha*:

> You should know that although I have taught many different aspects of the meditative states of hearers (those on the path to arhatship), bodhisattvas and tathagatas (Buddhas), these can all be included in the two practices of calm abiding and special insight.

## CALM ABIDING

Calm abiding is the ability to hold our minds on the object of meditation with clarity and stability for as long as we wish. With calm abiding, our minds become extremely flexible, giving us the liberty to focus on whatever virtuous object we wish. Although calm abiding alone can't cut the root of the disturbing attitudes, it drastically reduces their power. Gross anger, attachment and jealousy don't arise and consequently one feels more in harmony with the world.

For the mind to abide in a calm state, we must free it from

all worries, preconceptions, anxieties, and distractions. Thus, for the development of calm abiding, we do stabilizing meditation in which we train our minds to concentrate on the object of meditation.

The Buddha gave a variety of objects upon which we can focus to develop single-pointed concentration. These include meditating on love as the antidote to anger and on ugliness as the antidote to attachment. We could also meditate on the clear and aware nature of the mind. The image of the Buddha could be our meditation object, in which case we visualize the Buddha in our minds' eye and hold our concentration on this. One of the principal objects used to develop calm abiding is the breath.

To meditate on the breath, sit comfortably and breathe normally. Don't do deep breathing or force the breath in any way. Breathe as usual, only now observe and experience the breath fully. Focusing the attention at the tip of the nose, observe the sensation of the breath as you inhale and exhale.

Most of us are surprised and even alarmed when we start to meditate. It seems as if our minds resemble a street in downtown New York—there is so much noise, so many thoughts, so much push and pull. Meditation isn't causing our minds to be this cluttered. Actually, our minds are already racing around, but because our introspective awareness is weak, we aren't aware of it. This internal chatter isn't a hopeless situation, however. Through regular practice, our minds will be able to concentrate better and the distractions will diminish.

Laxity and agitation are the two principal hindrances to developing concentration. Laxity occurs when the mind is dull, and if it's not counteracted we can fall asleep. When the mind is sluggish, we should apply the proper antidotes to uplift it. We can temporarily stop focusing on the breath as the object of meditation and think about something that will raise our spirits, such as our perfect human rebirth or our potential to become a Buddha. It's also helpful to visualize clear light filling the room or bright light flooding into the body. This will enliven the mind and dispel the laxity. Then return to meditating on the breath.

For beginners who get sleepy when meditating, it's helpful to splash cold water on the face before sitting down. Between meditation sessions, looking long distances helps expand and invigorate the mind.

Agitation is the other chief obstacle to developing calm abiding. It occurs when the mind is attracted towards something we're attached to. For example, we focus on the breath for thirty seconds, and then, unbeknownst to us, our concentration strays to food. Then we think about our loved ones, and after that where we'll go on the weekend. These are all instances of agitation.

Agitation is different from distraction. The former is directed towards attractive objects that we're attached to, while the latter takes our attention to other things as well. For example, thinking about the insulting words someone snarled at us five years ago is an example of distraction. So is straying to thoughts of the Buddha's good qualities when we're supposed to be concentrating on the breath.

Agitation indicates that the mind is too high and excited. Thus, the antidote is to think about something somber. We can temporarily reflect on impermanence, the ugly aspects of whatever we're attached to or the suffering of cyclic existence. Having made our minds more serious, we then return to meditating on the breath.

Mindfulness and introspective alertness are two mental factors enabling us to prevent and counteract distraction, laxity and agitation. With mindfulness, we remember the object of meditation: the breath. Our memory or mindfulness of the breath is so strong that other distracting thoughts can't enter.

To ensure that we haven't become distracted, lax or agitated, introspective alertness is used to check whether or not we're still focused on the object of meditation. Introspective alertness is like a spy—it occasionally arises and quietly observes whether our mindfulness is still on the breath or whether it has strayed elsewhere. Introspective alertness also notices if our concentration is lax and not clearly focused on the breath.

If introspective alertness finds that we're still concentrating, we continue doing so. If it discovers we're distracted, lax or agitated, we then renew our mindfulness, bringing the mind back to the object of meditation. Or, we apply the antidotes to laxity and agitation described above.

Patience is another necessary quality for the development of calm abiding. We need to accept ourselves the way we are, and to have the confidence and enthusiasm to make our minds more peaceful. If we push ourselves and expect to receive immediate results, that attitude itself hinders us. On the other hand, if we're lazy, no progress is made. We need to cultivate relaxed effort.

Developing calm abiding is a gradual process that takes time. We shouldn't expect to meditate a few times and have single-pointed concentration. However, if we receive proper meditation instructions and follow them under the guidance of a teacher, and if we persist with joy and without expectation, we'll attain calm abiding.

## SPECIAL INSIGHT

Special insight is the correct discernment of the object of meditation coupled with the single-pointed concentration of calm abiding. To train in it, we need to develop the ability to analyze the meditation object. While stabilizing meditation is emphasized in the development of calm abiding, analytical meditation is instrumental to gain special insight. However, analytical meditation may also be used in the development of calm abiding, and stabilizing meditation contributes to special insight. In fact, special insight is a combination of analytical meditation and calm abiding.

Analytical or discerning meditation doesn't mean that we're constantly conceptualizing, thus getting lost in mental chatter. Rather, by understanding the object of meditation well, we'll be able to experience it fully. We aren't necessarily involved in discursive thought during analytical meditation. We may use more subtle thought to help us correctly discern the object. Then we concentrate on what we've discerned to make it firm and to integrate it with our minds. Eventually, our conceptual understanding will turn into direct experience. Thus the end product of analysis is non-conceptual experience. In *The Sutra Requested by Kasyapa*, the Buddha said:

> O Kasyapa, just as fire arises when two pieces of wood are rubbed against each other, so analytical wisdom arises from the conceptual state. And just as the fire increases and burns away all the wood, analytical wisdom increases and burns away all conceptual states.

There are two basic types of analytical meditation. In one we aim to transform our attitude. For example, when meditating on love, we change our attitude from anger or apathy into genuine affection. In the second, we analyze the meditation object in order to understand and perceive it. The meditations on impermanence and emptiness are examples.

In the first type of discerning meditation, we seek to transform our attitude. When meditating on love, the object of meditation is other beings. We consider their kindness towards us in the past, present and future. Letting ourselves absorb the profound implication of the fact that all others want to have happiness and avoid suffering as intensely as we do, we then reflect on how wonderful it would be if they could truly have happiness.

When these thoughts become strong our minds are filled with deep and impartial love for all others. A powerful feeling—the wish for others to have happiness—arises inside us. Having developed a loving attitude by using analysis, we then maintain this deep experience of love using stabilizing meditation. Some people may continue to meditate on love and develop calm abiding on it.

In the meditation on impermanence, analysis helps us to understand the transitory nature of our world. We can take something we're attached to—music, for example—and contemplate its quality of change. A melody has a beginning, middle and end. It doesn't continue forever. Even while it lasts, it's continuously changing. Each sound lasts a split second, and even in that short moment, it too changes.

When we consider impermanence deeply, we'll understand that our universe is always in motion. Although it appears firm and stable to our ordinary perception, in fact it's transient. Understanding this helps us avoid attachment and the pain and confusion which accompany it. Recognizing impermanence, we'll be able to appreciate things and experience them fully while they last. When they disappear, we won't mourn them. This automatically soothes mental turmoil in daily life.

When meditating on emptiness, we analyze the ultimate nature of people and phenomena. As described in the chapter on wisdom, we investigate whether our ordinary assumptions about how people and phenomena exist are correct. When we analyze carefully, we find that they are empty of all false projections of inherent existence. At this point, we've correctly discerned emptiness.

To attain special insight on emptiness, we conjoin our correct understanding of emptiness with calm abiding. This allows our minds to remain focused on emptiness for a long time. By concentrating on reality in this way, our minds are purified of obscurations.

All of the topics discussed in this book are topics for meditation. We can do analytical meditation on rebirth and cause and effect to understand how they function. Contemplating the kindness of others and the disadvantages of selfishness, we'll generate love and the spontaneous wish to benefit others. In short, everything the Buddha taught is food for meditation.

Both calm abiding and analytical meditation are important. If we just have the ability to concentrate, but we can't correctly analyze meditation objects such as emptiness, then we lack the ability to cut the root of ignorance. On the other hand, if we correctly understand emptiness but are unable to maintain our concentration on it, then our understanding won't have a deep impact on our minds and our ignorance won't be totally abolished. When we've conjoined calm abiding and special insight, then we're firmly on the path to freedom.

# 7 *Taking Refuge:*
## Resources on the path

A general understanding of the three principal realizations of the path gives us an excellent foundation for taking refuge in the Buddhas, Dharma and Sangha. When we have the determination to be free from difficulties, we'll seek a guide to show us how. When we genuinely cherish all beings, we'll seek someone to show us the most effective way to benefit them. As we recognize that the realization of emptiness is the key to freeing ourselves and to leading others to liberation, we'll yearn to receive proper instruction so we can meditate on emptiness.

The Buddhas, Dharma and Sangha are the Three Jewels of refuge. The Buddhas are all beings who have attained enlightenment; the Dharma is the realizations and teachings that lead us to liberation; the Sangha, in the strictest sense, refers to all those who have actualized this liberating wisdom by realizing emptiness directly.

Taking refuge in the Buddhas, the Dharma and the Sangha is the gateway to enter the path. Taking refuge implies taking responsibility for our own experience. Our happiness and suffering come from our own attitudes and actions. If we don't do anything to alter these, our situation won't change. However, we need to learn how to transform our attitudes and actions; we need others to show us the way to develop our good qualities. Others can't do the work for us, because only we can change our minds. Taking refuge means turning for guidance to the Buddhas, Dharma and Sangha with confidence that we can improve and with trust that they will guide us in the proper direction.

In this chapter we'll look at the qualities of the Three Jewels of refuge—the Buddhas, Dharma and Sangha—and will address the frequently asked question, "Do Buddhists believe in God?" Then the reasons people take refuge and the meaning of confidence (or faith) will be explored. The ways the Three Jewels can benefit us will be explained by analogy to a doctor, medicine and nurse; and lastly the refuge ceremony will be described.

## THE THREE JEWELS

What are the qualities of the Buddhas, Dharma and Sangha that make them reliable objects of refuge?

The Buddhas have completed the entire path to enlightenment and thus are able to show us the way. If we want to go to Hawaii, we should follow the instructions of someone who has been there. Otherwise, we could find ourselves in trouble! Since the journey to enlightenment is an even more delicate matter, it's essential that our guides have experienced it.

Shakyamuni Buddha is the particular Buddha who lived 2,500 years ago in India. (Sakya was his clan, Gotama his family name and Siddhartha his personal name.) There are other beings who have attained Buddhahood as well. "The Buddha" generally refers to Shakyamuni Buddha. However we shouldn't think of him as totally separate from other Buddhas, for they all have the same realizations.

Being omniscient, the Buddhas automatically know the most skillful way to guide each being to enlightenment. There are many stories in the sutras of how the Buddha guided people who were even worse off than we are.

One man, for example, was so stupid he couldn't even

remember the two words his tutor tried to teach him. Disgusted, the tutor threw him out. The man eventually met the Buddha, who gave him the job of sweeping the courtyard of the monks' assembly hall. The Buddha told him to say, "Remove dirt, remove stains," while he swept. After some time, the man realized the dirt and stains referred to weren't ordinary ones: dirt meant the mental obscurations to liberation and stains referred to the obscurations to full enlightenment. In this way, the man gained understanding of the path and eventually became an arhat or liberated being. If the Buddha has the skill to help someone like this, then he'll definitely be able to guide us!

The Buddhas have infinite, impartial compassion for all beings, so we can be assured of their continual help. Buddhas aren't like ordinary beings who help their friends and harm their enemies, or who help someone when she's nice, but not when she's in a bad mood. Rather, the Buddhas see beyond our superficial differences and weaknesses and have a constant, unbiased wish to help each of us.

A Buddha's ability to help others isn't limited by selfishness or ignorance. However, a Buddha can't make someone act in a certain way. Nor can the Buddhas counteract our karma. They can't erase the karmic imprints from our mindstreams or prevent them from ripening if all the necessary conditions are present. Buddhas can guide, inspire and teach us, but we're the only ones who can control our thoughts, words and deeds.

Just as the sun shines everywhere without discrimination or restriction, Buddhas help everyone equally. However, the sun's rays can't go into an upside-down pot. If the pot is on its side, a little light can go in. If it's upturned, then light floods into it.

Similarly, according to our attitudes and actions, we have different levels of receptivity to the enlightening influence of the Buddhas. A Buddha helps others effortlessly and spontaneously, but how much we receive depends on us. If we don't try to remedy our attachment, anger and closed-mindedness, we prevent ourselves from receiving the inspiration of the Buddhas. However, the more we follow the path, the more our minds automatically open to receive the Buddhas' inspiration and help.

Because our minds are obscured by disturbing attitudes and karma, we can't communicate directly with a Buddha's omniscient mind. Therefore, out of compassion, the Buddhas manifest in a variety of forms to guide us.

One form is called the enjoyment body. This is the subtle body a Buddha takes to teach the high bodhisattvas in the pure lands. Pure lands are places established by various Buddhas, where advanced practitioners can practice free of hindrances.

However, at the moment, our minds are so concerned with material things that we haven't yet created the causes to be born in pure lands. Therefore, out of compassion, Buddhas manifest in grosser bodies, appearing in our world in order to communicate with us. For example, a Buddha could manifest as our teacher, or as a Dharma friend. A Buddha could even appear as a bridge or an animal, or as a person who criticizes us in order to make us deal with our anger. However, the Buddhas don't announce what they're doing and we seldom recognize them.

Referring to the magnificent qualities of Shakyamuni Buddha, who lived 2,500 years ago in India, Buddhists praise his qualities:

> You, whose body was formed by a million perfect
> virtues,
> Whose speech fulfills the hopes of all beings,
> Whose mind perceives all that is to be known,
> To the prince of the Shakyas, we pay homage.

## THE DHARMA AND SANGHA

Dharma refers to two things: (1) the realizations of the path, particularly the wisdom directly realizing emptiness; and (2) the cessations of all sufferings and their causes brought about by these realizations.

The Dharma is our real protection. Once our minds have become the path and attain the cessations, no external or internal foe can harm us. In a more general sense, Dharma refers to the teachings of the Buddha that show us the way to actualize the realizations and cessations.

Sangha are all those who have directly realized emptiness. Thus, they are reliable friends who encourage and accompany us on the path. Strictly speaking, the term "Sangha" refers to anyone with direct realization of emptiness, be that person ordained or not. Included in the Sangha are arhats, those who have freed themselves from cyclic existence. Bodhisattvas who have directly realized emptiness are also Sangha. These noble bodhisattvas have control over their rebirth process. Due to their great compassion, they continuously and voluntarily return to our world to guide us.

More commonly, "sangha" refers to the communities of monks and nuns who have dedicated their lives to actualizing the Dharma, although they may not yet have attained realizations. In the West, some people use "sangha" to refer to the community of lay followers as well. However, this is not the traditional usage of the word.


## DO BUDDHISTS BELIEVE IN GOD?

People from Judeo-Christian backgrounds often ask if Buddhists believe in God. This depends on what is meant by the word "God," for there is a diversity of opinions in the Judeo-Christian world about who or what God is.

If by the word "God" we refer to the principle of love and compassion, then yes, Buddhists accept those principles. Love and compassion are the essential core of the Buddha's teachings. Many similarities exist between Jesus' and Buddha's teachings in this regard.

If we take "God" to refer to one who has infinite love and wisdom and who is free of vengeance and partiality, then yes, Buddhists accept this. Love, wisdom, patience and impartiality are qualities of all the Buddhas.

If "God" is used to refer to a creator, then Buddhists have a differing view. From a Buddhist viewpoint, there was no beginning to the continuities of physical matter and consciousness (see the chapter on rebirth). Since many logical difficulties arise if the existence of a creator is posited, Buddhists propose an alternative explanation. Thus, Buddhists don't accept the ideas of original sin or eternal damnation. Nor is faith alone sufficient to attain peace.

It must be emphasized, however, that Buddhists see the plurality of religious beliefs and practices as beneficial. Since people don't think in the same way, a diversity of beliefs enables each person to select a system that helps him or her to live a better life. Thus, Buddhists emphasize the importance and necessity of religious tolerance.

## WHY TAKE REFUGE?

Two principal attitudes cause us to turn to the Three Jewels for refuge. These attitudes also help to deepen our refuge as time goes on. These are: (1) dread of continuing the way we are, and (2) confidence in the abilities of the Three Jewels to guide us.

Realizing how often our disturbing attitudes overwhelm us, we fear they'll propel us towards unhappiness now and an unfortunate rebirth in the future. Looking even further ahead, we dread being trapped in cyclic existence, taking one uncontrolled rebirth after another. We know that no matter where we're born, there's no lasting happiness.

Because we don't know how to solve these dilemmas, we must seek advice from those who do. But we must be careful about whose instructions we follow, for if we pick a guide who is limited in compassion, wisdom and skill, we won't be able to improve. Thus, it's essential to examine closely the qualities of possible sources of help. When we have confidence in the abilities of another to guide us, then we'll listen to their instructions and practice what we learn.

## CONFIDENCE VERSUS BLIND FAITH

The term "confidence" in Buddhist scriptures is often translated as faith. However, the English word "faith" has connotations of someone who believes in something but doesn't know why. Blind faith of this sort isn't cultivated in Buddhism. "Confidence" expresses the meaning better: we know about the Buddhas, Dharma and Sangha and we trust their ability to help us. Three kinds of constructive faith or confidence are developed in Buddhist practice: (1) convinced confidence, (2) aspiring confidence, and (3) admiring or clear confidence.

Convinced confidence arises from understanding. For example, we hear about the disadvantages of the disturbing attitudes and learn techniques to overcome them. We then examine our lives to see if disturbing attitudes cause us problems and if the techniques effectively counteract them. In this way, we'll develop conviction that it's necessary and possible to eliminate the disturbing attitudes. Through reason and our own experience, we'll become convinced that contemplating impermanence will diminish our unreasonable attachments. Because this kind of faith is based on understanding, it's firm and valid.

We can gain convinced confidence that the Buddhas, Dharma and Sangha are able to lead us from our confusion. We don't need to believe in the greatness of the Three Jewels just because someone told us to, for that would be like buying a laundry soap simply because the commercial said it was good. Rather, through learning and reflecting on the qualities of the Three Jewels, we'll understand and will be convinced. Such conviction makes us feel close to the Buddhas, Dharma and Sangha.

Aspiring confidence is the second kind of confidence. Reading about the benefits of a kind heart and observing the wonderful effects altruistic people have upon the world, we'll aspire to increase our love and compassion. Learning about our Buddha nature and the qualities of the Three Jewels, we'll aspire to become Buddhas. This kind of faith is very invigorating and gives us enthusiasm for the Dharma practice.

Clear or admiring confidence makes our minds joyful. For example, we hear about the qualities of the bodhisattvas and Buddhas—their impartial compassion and penetrating wisdom—and admire them with a happy heart. By focusing on others' good qualities and rejoicing, admiring confidence arises within us.

Confidence in the Buddhas, Dharma and Sangha makes our hearts peaceful and gives direction to our lives. As the Buddha said in the *Dhammapada*:

> The wise take faith and intelligence
> For their security in life;
> These are their finest wealth.
> That other wealth is just commonplace.

In Buddhism, faith or confidence is developed slowly, and it arises through knowledge and understanding. By relying on the guidance of the Buddhas, Dharma and Sangha, our understanding of the three principal realizations of the path will grow. Conversely, by deepening our inner understanding and transforming our minds, our confidence in and reliance upon the Three Jewels increase. This occurs because we discern through our own experience that the direction provided by the Three Jewels resolves our unsatisfactory situations. In this way, taking refuge involves taking responsibility for our own experience, as well as relying on the guidance, instruction and inspiration of those who can show us the way to transform our minds.

## DOCTOR, MEDICINE AND NURSE

Refuge is likened to the doctor, medicine and nurse a sick person relies upon to be cured. We're like a sick person because we're afflicted with many unsatisfactory situations in this and future lives. Seeking a solution, we consult a qualified doctor, the Buddha. The Buddha diagnoses the cause of our illness: the disturbing attitudes and the confused actions we've done under their influence. Then he prescribes the medicine of the Dharma, the teachings on how to gain the realizations and cessations leading to enlightenment.

We must practice the teachings to attain the result. It isn't sufficient just to hear the Dharma. We have to actively apply it in our daily lives and in our relationships with others. This means we try to be mindful and notice when disturbing attitudes arise. Then, we apply the remedies enabling us to perceive the situation clearly. If sick people have medicine but don't take it, they aren't cured. Similarly, we may have an elaborate shrine at home and a huge library of Dharma books, but if we don't apply patience when we meet a person who annoys us, we've missed the opportunity to practice.

The Sangha are like the nurses who help us take the medicine. Sometimes we forget which pills to take when, so the nurses remind us. If we have difficulty swallowing huge pills, the nurses break them into bits for us. Similarly, those with realizations of the path are the real Sangha who help us practice the Dharma correctly when we get confused. Monks and nuns provide a good example, and any practitioner who is more advanced than we are can help us.

Our Dharma friends are very important, for we're easily influenced by the people we're around. When we're trying to improve ourselves, it's important to be around people who encourage us in this pursuit. If we spend time with people who enjoy gossiping and criticizing others, that's what we're likely to do when we're with them. When we're near people who value self-cultivation, their example and encouragement will influence us positively. For that reason the Buddha said in the *Dhammapada*:

> Wise ones, do not befriend
> The faithless, who are mean
> And slanderous and cause schism.
> Don't take bad people as your companions.

Wise ones, be intimate
With the faithful who speak gently,
Are ethical and do much listening.
Take the best as companions.

How are we to link this advice with our effort to develop impartial love and compassion for everyone? Mentally, we try to look beyond people's superficial qualities and cherish them all equally. However, as we aren't yet Buddhas, we're still easily influenced by others.

Thus, for the benefit of everyone, it's wiser to form friendships with people who live ethically and value self-cultivation. Although mentally we can have equal love and compassion for everyone, physically we should remain near those who influence us positively. When our own minds become stronger, then we can be around anyone without being influenced by his or her bad habits.

## THE REFUGE CEREMONY

Although taking refuge is done in our hearts and doesn't require a ritual, participating in the refuge-taking ceremony allows us to receive the inspiration of the lineage of practitioners that began with the Buddha and continues down to the present. Also, we're formally entrusting ourselves to the guidance of the Three Jewels.

By taking refuge, we're making a firm statement to ourselves and to the holy beings that we'll take a beneficial direction in life. We're determined to stop letting our selfishness and ignorance fool us into chasing after useless pursuits. Instead, we'll get in touch with our inner wisdom and compassion. Making this decision and taking refuge is a very precious moment in our lives, for we are embarking on the path to enlightenment.

In the Tibetan tradition this verse of taking refuge and generating the altruistic intention is recited in the morning upon awaking and before all meditation sessions:

I go for refuge, until I am enlightened, to the Buddhas, the Dharma and the Sangha. By the positive potential I create by practicing generosity and the other far-reaching attitudes (ethics, patience, joyous effort, meditative stabilization and wisdom), may I attain Buddhahood in order to benefit all beings.

# PART VI

# HISTORY AND TRADITIONS

# 1 The Buddha's Life and the Growth of Buddhism:
## Siddhartha's enlightenment and the spread of his teaching

*. . . these discourses (of the Buddha) unconsciously portray for us the first distinct character of India's history: a man of strong will, authoritative and proud, but of gentle manner and speech, and of infinite benevolence. He claimed enlightenment but not inspiration; he never pretended that a god was speaking through him. In controversy he was more patient and considerate than any other of the great teachers of mankind. . . . Like Lao-tze and Christ he wished to return good for evil, love for hate; and he remained silent under misunderstanding and abuse. . . . Unlike most saints, Buddha had a sense of humor, and knew that metaphysics without laughter is immodesty.*
> —*Will Durant (1885-1981), American historian and Pulitzer Prize winner*

Many auspicious signs greeted Prince Siddhartha, who was born to the royal couple of Kapilavastu in the sixth century B.C.E. Rainbows appeared in the sky, animals were at peace, and there was great happiness throughout the land. Before Siddhartha's birth, his mother had many auspicious dreams, and the child was indeed remarkable. As a newborn infant, he took seven steps and declared this was his last rebirth.

From the beginning, Prince Siddhartha excelled in intellectual and athletic pursuits. Prohibited by his father from venturing beyond the palace gates, he led a very sheltered life. He married, had a child, and spent his time enjoying the delights of royal life.

But the prince was interested in how people lived, and so unbeknownst to his parents, he left the palace with his charioteer on several occasions. To his horror, he came across unexpected sights: a sick person, an old person and a corpse. His charioteer explained to the shocked prince that sickness, aging and death come to everyone without choice.

On another visit Prince Siddhartha saw a wandering mendicant. He learned that this penniless holy person was seeking true understanding of life and liberation from its difficulties. After these experiences, the prince began to reconsider the purpose of his own life.

Siddhartha began to feel restless among the palace pleasures and desired to find a solution to life's problems, answers to his questions about life and death. Unable to tolerate the meaningless frivolity of palace life any more, he decided to dedicate his life to spiritual pursuits. One night he left the palace, and shedding his royal clothes and ornaments, became a mendicant.

Although he studied with the greatest meditation masters of that time and accomplished all they taught, he still hadn't discovered the nature of reality, nor found his way out of cyclic existence. Then, for six agonizing years, he sought realizations through asceticism. Finally understanding that torturing the body doesn't purify the mind, he abandoned this practice. Then, sitting under a bodhi tree in the village of Bodh Gaya in northern India, he vowed not to arise until he had attained full enlightenment.

Many forces, internal and external, tried to distract him from his meditation. But at dawn of the full moon in the fourth lunar month, he succeeded in freeing his mind from all obscurations and developing all of his potential. He became a fully enlightened Buddha.

For forty-five years, the Buddha then taught all over northern India and what is today part of Nepal. Men and women wished to take ordination from him, and thus the sangha communities of monks and nuns began. Laymen and women also studied with the Buddha and took the five lay precepts (not to kill, steal, have unwise sexual relations, lie or take intoxicants). The lay followers donated parks so the sangha would have dwelling places and supplied the monks and nuns with their food, clothing and medicine. The sangha lived simply, practiced well and taught the Dharma.

After several years, the Buddha returned to Kapilavastu to teach the Dharma to his family. His son became a monk and his aunt, who had raised him after his mother's death, became the first nun. His wife and son entered the sangha. His father the king and the rest of the kingdom also followed the Buddha's teachings.

In many ways, the Buddha changed Indian society. He discouraged excessive ritual and encouraged people to understand the ceremonies they participate in. Indian society was enmeshed in the prejudice of the caste system, but the Buddha prohibited the caste system among his followers. In Indian society, women were kept at home and given little freedom. However, the Buddha acknowledged women's ability to attain liberation and encouraged them to assume "the homeless life" of a nun. He encouraged the sangha to operate in a democratic way, creating a model that ultimately changed the manner of even the secular government at that time.

The Buddha's life and his philosophy have influenced the world ever since. It led Mahatma Gandhi, who led India to freedom from British colonialism, to say:

> I have no hesitation in declaring that I owe a great deal
> to the inspiration that I have derived from the life of

the Enlightened One. . . . His love, his boundless love
went out as much to the lower animal, to the lowest
life as to human beings. And he insisted upon purity
of life.


## THE SPREAD OF BUDDHISM

Shortly after the Buddha's passing away, or parinirvana, five
hundred arhats met and recited the Buddhas' discourses to
preserve and systematize them. These sutras were memorized
and passed down orally for centuries, until they were written
down in Ceylon around the second century B.C.E., forming
the Pali Canon of the Theravada tradition.

The Buddha gave other teachings during his lifetime that
were passed down privately from teacher to disciple in the early
centuries after his passing away. It's said that some of these
teachings, the *Prajna-paramita Sutras*, were hidden until the
circumstances were ripe for them to spread. Centuries later,
the sage Nagarjuna revived them. These Mahayana sutras, written in Sanskrit, began to appear in the first century B.C.E.,
and rapidly became popular.

In the sixth century the tantras, another group of Buddha's
teachings, appeared in writing. According to the Vajrayana tradition, these teachings were given by the Buddha during his
lifetime. Because they were too advanced to be taught to public audiences, they were passed down quietly from master to
disciple for centuries or taken to other places for protection.

After the Buddha's passing, his teachings spread rapidly
across India to present-day Pakistan and Afghanistan. Remains
of this great Buddhist civilization can be seen at the Ajanta
and Ellora caves in India, with their elaborate sculpture and
painting, and at Bamiyan in Afghanistan where huge Buddha
images were carved into the sides of a mountain. Buddhist
monastic universities were established in India and were the
center of intellectual thought for centuries. The ruins of
Nalanda, the foremost of these, can be seen in Bihar today.

Active practice of Buddha's teachings disappeared from Indian culture after the twelfth century when Buddhism was virtually destroyed by Muslim invaders. However, the Buddhist influence on Indian culture remained, and there has been a resurgence of active Buddhist practice in recent years. Many Indian "untouchables" have become Buddhist. The group of 500,000 who converted in 1956 has now swelled to nearly six million.

The other large group of Buddhists in India are Tibetan refugees. After 1959 thousands of Tibetans, including His Holiness the Dalai Lama, fled to India in order to escape the Chinese communist takeover of their country. The Indian government did much to help the refugees, enabling them to preserve the teachings and religious institutions that have met with severe repression in Tibet under communist rule.

India was the root from which Buddhism spread all over Asia. In the third century B.C.E. King Ashoka sent missionaries to Ceylon (Sri Lanka), where Buddhism took root. From both Ceylon and India, Buddhism spread to Thailand and Burma and down the Southeast Asian peninsula. The teachings went there in waves, first the Theravada, then Mahayana and finally Vajrayana. By the seventh century, Buddhism reached Indonesia, where the famous Borobudur Stupa was built.

In most of Southeast Asia—Thailand, Burma and Cambodia—the Theravada tradition became dominant and continues to be so. However in Vietnam, Theravada, Ch'an (Zen) and Pure Land traditions are found. In Malaysia and Indonesia, Buddhism diminished after the Muslim invasions of the fourteenth century. However, Chinese immigrants to Malaya in the last century brought Buddhism with them, and several Buddhist traditions are present in modern Malaysia and Singapore. Small groups of Buddhists remain in Indonesia.

Around the third century B.C.E. Buddhism spread to the Central Asian kingdoms and was carried along the silk route. It came to China from Central Asia and also from India by sea. Chinese pilgrims went to India and brought back many scriptures which were translated into Chinese. By the fourth century C.E. Buddhism was strong in China.

Many sutras were brought to China by different people over the centuries, but they weren't systematized. Therefore after a while some confusion arose about how to harmonize seeming discrepancies among sutras and about how to practice what was contained in this vast amount of literature. To resolve this difficulty, small groups arose, each led by a prominent monk. Each group took as its focal point a particular sutra or group of sutras. Thus various Buddhist traditions developed in China. Pure Land and Ch'an (Zen) became the most popular. The earliest Buddhist schools as well as the later Vajrayana teachings also traveled to China, but they weren't widespread.

From China, these various traditions spread to Korea beginning in the fourth century. From there, they went to Japan, where Buddhism was well established by the ninth century. Several Buddhist traditions now exist in Japan: Pure Land, Zen, Nichiren and Shingon, which is a tantric tradition. From China, Buddhism also spread southward into Vietnam.

Buddhism initially entered Tibet in the seventh century from Nepal and China. Padmasambhava, the great Indian yogi, came to Tibet in the ninth century and Buddhism spread rapidly. After a famous debate between the Indian sage Kamalasila and a Chinese proponent of Ch'an, the Tibetans turned to India as their source for Buddhism. Four major traditions of Tibetan Buddhism arose, mostly due to different lineages of teachings. Their manner of practice is similar. From Tibet, Buddhism spread to Mongolia, North China and parts of the Soviet Union, as well as throughout the Himalayan region.

Although King Ashoka sent Buddhist missionaries to Greece in the third century B.C.E., Buddhism didn't really become known to the West until the last century.

Interestingly, there seem to be indications that the ''lost years'' of Jesus' early life were spent in India. A scripture was found in a Buddhist monastery in Ladakh, north India, telling of a young man who studied there and later returned to his own country. The dates and description in the text were similar to that of Jesus' life, but more historical research is needed before any conclusion can be drawn. However, there's a striking resemblance between Jesus' teachings on love and compassion and those of the Buddha.

In the nineteenth century some Western intellectuals became interested in Buddhist teachings and Buddhist philosophy began to be taught in the universities. In recent years Westerners have shown an increased interest in Buddhism, and now all major Buddhist traditions have temples and centers in most Western countries.

Buddhism has inspired many people in the West spiritually and intellectually. People in modern Western societies appreciate the meditation techniques the Buddha taught for calming the mind. They're inspired by Buddhism's clear instructions on how to develop love and compassion. Intellectually, people are stimulated by Buddhism's logical and open-minded approach.

In addition, the Buddhist approach is similar to the scientific method and its world view is harmonious with scientific discoveries. Erich Fromm, the German-American psychoanalyst and social philosopher said:

> Paradoxically, Eastern religious thought turns out to be more congenial to Western rational thought than does Western religious thought itself.

The eminent British judge, Christmas Humphreys, commented:

> Buddhism...is a system of thought, a religion, a spiritual science and a way of life which is reasonable, practical and all-embracing. For 2,500 years it has satisfied the spiritual needs of nearly one-third of mankind. It appeals to those in search of truth because it has no dogmas, satisfies the reason and the heart alike, insists on self-reliance coupled with tolerance for other points of view, embraces science, religion, philosophy, psychology, mysticism, ethics and art, and points to man alone as the creator of his present life and sole designer of his destiny.

# 2 A Survey of Buddhist Traditions Today: Unity and diversity

The Buddha, who was a very skillful teacher, gave a variety of teachings suitable for people of different interests and inclinations. Not everyone is expected to practice in the same way, and thus Buddhists welcome the diversity of Buddhist traditions as well as the diversity of religions in the world.

Although Buddhism is one of the oldest religions, there has never been a war fought in its name or over its doctrine. Sectarianism is considered extremely destructive, for to say one tradition is good and another is bad is to criticize the teaching the Buddha gave to a particular group of people.

That doesn't contradict the benefit of debate among the traditions, or even between two practitioners of the same tradition. Buddhist debate is done with the positive motivation of increasing the participants' understanding. By debating, students think more deeply and iron out their own and their debate partner's misunderstandings. Thus Buddhist masters encourage their students to question and discuss the teachings.

Newcomers are sometimes confused by the variety of Buddhist traditions. Therefore a brief explanation follows, although it doesn't do justice to the richness of the traditions. Although there are many Buddhist traditions, here only the practices of the most prominent are discussed: Theravada, Pure Land, Zen and Vajrayana.

## THERAVADA

The Theravada, or Tradition of the Elders, emphasizes two meditation practices: samatha (calm abiding) and vipassana (special insight). The practice of calm abiding develops concentration, ceasing the torrent of chattering thoughts and engendering the ability to focus on the meditation object single-pointedly. The in-and-out flow of the breath is the primary object used in this meditation, and developing concentration upon it leads to a serenely settled state of mind.

Special insight is cultivated through the four mindfulnesses: observing the body, feelings, mind and phenomena. One gains insight into their impermanence, problematic nature and lack of self-identity.

Another practice, loving-kindness meditation, is done to develop a sincere wish for everyone to be well and happy. In addition, the Theravada tradition encourages keeping precepts: either the five precepts of a lay practitioner or the vows of a monk or nun.

In the intervals between meditation sessions, Theravada practitioners do walking meditation. By walking extremely slowly, they maintain mindfulness of every movement. This is a very useful technique to anchor one in the present moment and make one more attentive to what is happening here and now. The Theravada tradition aims at attaining arhatship, liberation from cyclic existence.

## PURE LAND

The Pure Land tradition stresses the practice of Buddha Amitabha: chanting his name and meditating on him. Practitioners of this tradition seek rebirth in Sukhavati, the Western Pure Land, where all conditions necessary for Dharma practice are readily available. Having been reborn there, they'll be able to complete the path and attain Buddhahood without hindrance.

To be reborn in Sukhavati, Pure Land practitioners imagine Amitabha, contemplate his enlightened qualities and chant his name. In addition, they try to live ethically and to develop the altruistic intention. To gain calm abiding they concentrate single-pointedly on the visualized image of Amitabha, and to develop special insight, they analyze the ultimate nature of Amitabha and themselves.

Pure Land, Zen (Ch'an) and Vajrayana are all Mahayana traditions. Therefore the practitioners aim to become Buddhas, and the bodhisattva precepts are given to those who wish. Nowadays, the practices of Pure Land and Zen have been blended in many temples.


## ZEN

Zen emphasizes that all beings have the Buddha nature. Thus, if someone cuts through all false conceptualization and realizes the empty nature of the mind, he or she will become Buddha in this lifetime. Zen practitioners meditate on the breath and also on the mind.

Zen is rich with short stories that can be contemplated at length. One of my favorites is about Bankei, a Zen master conducting a meditation retreat. A student was caught stealing, and the incident was reported to Bankei with a request that the person be expelled. Bankei ignored the request. This happened again and was similarly ignored. Angered, the other students submitted a petition asking that the culprit be dismissed and stating that they would leave if he weren't.

Bankei called everyone together and said, "You are wise. You know what is right and wrong. You may go somewhere else to study if you wish. But this poor student doesn't even know right from wrong. If I don't teach him, who will? I want him to stay here even if the rest of you leave."

At that point, the student who had stolen began to cry. He no longer had any desire to steal.

Within Zen, there are two traditions. Soto Zen does the practice of "just sitting" to develop calm abiding and special insight into the workings and nature of the mind. Practitioners of Rinzai Zen contemplate koans, sayings that are incomprehensible to the ordinary intellect and emotions. Understanding a koan requires freeing the mind of ordinary views. An example is the following:

> Two monks were arguing about a flag. One said the flag was moving. The other said the wind was moving. The Sixth Patriarch passed by and told them, "Not the wind, not the flag; the mind is moving."

Zen practitioners are encouraged to do physical work, this being a chance to apply what is gained in meditation to daily activities. Zen also uses artistic expression as an opportunity to develop mindfulness, and in this atmosphere the exquisite practices of the tea ceremony and flower arrangement have developed.

In places where Ch'an from China is practiced, the monks and nuns are celibate. However, in Japan the government wanted the sangha to marry, and in the last half of the nineteenth century it ordered the abolition of the celibacy requirement. Thus in Japan Zen priests may marry, for their system of vows is different from that of other Buddhist traditions.


## VAJRAYANA

The Vajrayana, or Tantra, is practiced by Tibetan Buddhists and also the Japanese Shingon tradition. Vajrayana practice is based on the three principal realizations of the path: the determination to be free, the altruistic intention and the wisdom realizing emptiness. Vajrayana is a branch of the Mahayana, which in turn is based on the Theravada. One can't jump over the initial practices which are in common with the Theravada and general Mahayana, and directly enter the Vajrayana. If one ignores the three principal realizations and instead has the fanciful attitude, "I'm going to practice Vajrayana because it's the highest and quickest way to enlightenment," then one's practice won't bear the desired fruits.

This is an important point, for nowadays many people are enchanted with the idea of gaining special powers and seek the tantra for that reason. However, such a motivation isn't the proper one. The Vajrayana practice isn't for worldly power and fame. It's done to attain enlightenment and thus be able to benefit others most effectively.

To undertake the Vajrayana practice, one's mind must be well-trained in the preliminary subjects. These include meditation on death and impermanence, the Four Noble Truths, the determination to be free, the altruistic intention and the wisdom realizing emptiness. By first training in the basic meditations, one becomes a suitable vessel for receiving empowerment into a tantric practice.

One enters the Vajrayana by taking an empowerment (often called initiation) from a qualified master. During an empowerment, the master gives instruction on how to meditate, and the disciples do the meditation. Just sitting in the room and drinking blessed water isn't taking an empowerment. The purpose of an empowerment is to help the students make a connection with a particular manifestation of the Buddha and introduce them to the meditation practice of that Buddha. It is extremely important to keep the vows and commitments taken during an empowerment.

After the empowerment, one asks a qualified teacher for instructions on the vows and commitments taken during the empowerment. Teachings on that meditation practice may also be requested. One receives a sadhana, a ritual text with the visualizations, prayers and meditation of that Buddha, and the spiritual master gives instructions on it. Having received these instructions, one does the meditation properly.

The Vajrayana emphasizes developing a positive self-image. In ordinary life, if we can't imagine graduating from school, we'll never try to and we'll never do it. Similarly, if we can't imagine becoming a Buddha, we'll never become one. The visualizations done in the Vajrayana practice help us to develop a positive self-image and to expand our altruistic intention.

There are several meditation techniques found in the Vajrayana. Certain preliminary practices purify negative imprints and build up positive potentials. The recitation of mantras calms the mind and aids in the development of concentration. Within the Vajrayana are also found techniques for quickly developing single-pointed concentration and for making manifest an extremely subtle state of mind that realizes emptiness. Vajrayana also includes meditations to transform the death and rebirth process into the path to enlightenment.

All of these meditations are based on an understanding of the three principal aspects of the path. By practicing such a gradual path to enlightenment, we can totally eliminate all defilements from our minds and transform them into the minds of Buddhas. With perfectly developed compassion, wisdom and skillful means, we'll be able to benefit others extensively.

# PART VII

# COMPASSION IN ACTION

# Compassion in Action

Thus far we've discussed new approaches to life and to our relations with other people. For these to be valuable, they must relate to our daily lives. This book hasn't been written for the sake of intellectual knowledge, but to offer some ideas that could be helpful in making our lives richer.

As His Holiness the Dalai Lama says repeatedly, the key element in a happy life and in a harmonious society is compassion. Compassion, the essence of the Buddha's teachings, is also encouraged by all of the world's religions.

Compassion is honest and direct communication with others. It's the ability to understand others and to spontaneously help them the same way as we help ourselves. Because the sense of "I" and "other" is reduced, compassion is imbued with humility. Because the wish to free others from unsatisfactory conditions is strong, compassion is courageous.

His Holiness the Dalai Lama exemplifies these qualities. During a conference with psychologists and others in the helping professions in 1989, he astonished everyone with his humility. He sometimes responded to difficult questions with "I don't know. What do you think?" In a world where the famous often portray themselves as authorities, His Holiness' respect for others' opinions and his openness to learn from them indicates a bright alternative.

Similarly, he lives courageous compassion. His country, Tibet, has been occupied by the Chinese communists since 1949. In 1959, His Holiness, along with thousands of Tibetans, were forced into exile. The Cultural Revolution inflicted massive destruction on Tibetan society, religion and people. Yet, His Holiness constantly advises the Tibetans, "Do not be angry at those who destroyed our homeland. They are living beings who want to be happy just as we do. Violent opposition to them doesn't remedy the situation."

While being compassionate towards those who have occupied Tibet, His Holiness is nevertheless courageous in working to remedy the plight of his people. He is actively seeking a peaceful solution that would be satisfactory to the Chinese and the Tibetans. Thus, we see in his life the harmonious blend of compassion, humility and courage.

We can apply the Dalai Lama's example to our own lives. Each situation we encounter provides an opportunity to practice compassionate action. We start with the people around us—our family and friends, colleagues and classmates, people in the grocery store and on the road—and spread our care and concern to all.

When someone cuts us off on the highway, instead of swearing in anger, we can put ourselves in that person's shoes. We've been inconsiderate drivers sometimes, usually because we've been preoccupied with something important. The other person is similar. Just as we want others to excuse our mistakes, so too can we forgive theirs.

We can learn to apply the affection we feel for our family and friends to others. We want our children and parents to be happy. Others may not be our relatives, but they are someone's parents and children. They are the same in being parents and children, only the possessive pronoun describing them is different: "their" instead of "our." Once we recognize the arbitrariness of these labels "mine" and "others," our love and compassion can spread to everyone impartially. In this way, feelings of alienation and barriers between people fall away.

How can we love people who are considered "evil" by society? No person is inherently and thoroughly evil. Everyone has the potential to become a Buddha. The clouds of their confusion and violent anger and desire obscure their basic goodness.

Loving a criminal, for example, doesn't mean we let him continue harming others. Compassion for both the victims and perpetrators of harmful actions is needed. Not wanting the perpetrators to create destructive actions that cause their own future suffering, we should stop them. Thus, without hatred or vengeance, we can compassionately extend help to all parties in a bad situation.

Having compassion for all beings equally doesn't mean we neglect our family and friends. Some people become so involved in improving society that their own children develop problems due to lack of parental guidance. It's easy to take those with whom we live for granted. However, we mustn't forget that our family and friends are beings whom we can benefit too.

## HELPING OUR COMPASSION TO GROW DAILY

Just telling ourselves to be patient or compassionate doesn't make those attitudes arise in our minds. They need to be deliberately cultivated. Therefore, it's important to keep aside some "quiet time" each day to work on our inner well-being.

A few minutes of quiet time in the morning allows us to set the motivation not to harm others and to help them as much as possible during the day. Quiet time in the evening gives us the opportunity to review and "digest" the day's events. Observing our reactions to what happened during the day helps us to get to know ourselves. We may observe that we're very sensitive to criticism or feel imposed upon when others ask for our help. We then can ask ourselves if we want to continue having those attitudes and feelings. If we don't, we can apply the techniques suggested in this book to change them.

There needn't be a dualistic split between our quiet self-cultivation and our activities with others. Alone, we can reflect on our lives and actions and determine how we want to act with others. At work, we'll integrate and practice that. Later we'll reflect on what happened at work, learn from our experiences and make new determinations for the future. In this way, our quiet time for Dharma practice and our daily activities complement each other. We grow from and in each of them.

Consistency is important in self-cultivation. It's far better to set aside ten minutes every day than to meditate for five hours once a month. However, if we're able to, spending a few days or weeks each year doing meditation retreat is valuable. At that time, we're able to go deeper into the process of personal development.

People in modern societies have very busy lives, and it's easy to be distracted from self-cultivation. However, if we establish our priorities clearly, keeping time for internal reflection becomes easier. For example, we consider all the activities we could become involved in and list them in order of their importance to us. By this, we gain the clarity and the strength needed to arrange our daily schedule in a more manageable way.

It's important to set realistic goals for our spiritual practice and not expect ourselves to change immediately. External conditions in modern societies may change quickly, but our attitudes and habits don't. Patience with ourselves as well as with others is necessary. If we are judgmental and hard on ourselves, we surely will be that way with others. But such an attitude doesn't help ourselves or others to change. If we love and are patient with ourselves, we'll gradually improve. Similarly, if we have those attitudes towards others, we won't be demanding or impatient.

Balance is essential. Sometimes we need to stretch our limits. Other times we need to be quiet and absorb what we've learned. We have to be sensitive to our needs at any particular moment and act accordingly. Finding a middle way between the extremes of pushing ourselves to do more than we're capable of and being self-indulgent and lazy is a constant challenge.

As we become more skillful in balancing our activities, we'll be able to avoid "burn-out." People in the helping professions and people with busy lives face the danger of over-extending themselves. Sometimes it's hard to say, "No, I'm sorry. Although that project is very valuable, I can't help you with it right now." We may feel guilty or lazy, as if we're letting others down.

However, taking on more than we're capable of helps neither ourselves nor others. We need to assess our abilities accurately. Sometimes we may be able to engage in many projects. Other times, more quiet reflection and study are needed. If we take this time, we'll be refreshed and then will be able to spend more quality time with others. As one of my teachers, Lama Yeshe, advised:

> It is important to understand that true practice is something we do from moment to moment, from day to day. We do whatever we can, with whatever wisdom we have, and dedicate it all to the benefit of others. We just live our life simply, to the best of our ability. This in itself will be of enormous benefit to others; we don't need to wait until we become Buddhas before we can begin to act.

# Glossary

ALTRUISTIC INTENTION (BODHICITTA): the mind dedicated to attaining enlightenment in order to be able to benefit all others most effectively.

ARHAT: a person who has attained liberation and is thus free from cyclic existence.

ATTACHMENT: an attitude that exaggerates the good qualities of a person or thing and then clings to it.

BODHICITTA: see altruistic intention.

BODHISATTVA: a person who has developed the spontaneous altruistic intention.

BUDDHA: any person who has purified all defilements and developed all good qualities. "The Buddha" refers to Shakyamuni Buddha, who lived 2,500 years ago in India.

BUDDHA NATURE (BUDDHA POTENTIAL): the factors allowing all beings to attain full enlightenment.

CALM ABIDING: the ability to remain single-pointedly on the object of meditation with a pliant and blissful mind.

COMPASSION: the wish for all others to be free from suffering and its causes.

CYCLIC EXISTENCE: taking uncontrolled rebirth under the influence of disturbing attitudes and karmic imprints.

DETERMINATION TO BE FREE: the attitude aspiring to be free from all problems and sufferings and to attain liberation.

DHARMA: in the most general sense, Dharma refers to the teachings and doctrine of the Buddha. More specifically, it refers to the realizations of the path and the consequent cessations of suffering and its causes.

DISTURBING ATTITUDES: attitudes such as ignorance, attachment, anger, pride, jealousy, and closed-mindedness, which disturb our mental peace and propel us to act in ways harmful to others.

EMPTINESS: the lack of independent or inherent existence. This is the ultimate nature or reality of all persons and phenomena.

ENLIGHTENMENT (BUDDHAHOOD): the state of a Buddha, i.e. the state of having forever eliminated all disturbing attitudes, karmic imprints and their stains from one's mindstream, and having developed one's good qualities and wisdom to their fullest extent. Buddhahood supersedes liberation.

IMPUTE: to give a label or name to an object; to attribute meaning to an object.

INHERENT OR INDEPENDENT EXISTENCE: a false and non-existent quality that we project onto persons and phenomena; existence independent of causes and conditions, parts or the mind labeling a phenomenon.

KARMA: intentional action. Our actions leave imprints on our mindstreams which bring about our experiences.

LIBERATION: the state of having removed all disturbing attitudes and karma causing us to take rebirth in cyclic existence.

LOVE: the wish for all others to have happiness and its causes.

MAHAYANA: the Buddhist tradition that asserts that all beings can attain enlightenment. It strongly emphasizes the development of compassion and the altruistic intention.

MANTRA: a series of syllables consecrated by a Buddha and expressing the essence of the entire path to enlightenment. Mantras can be recited during meditation to calm and purify the mind.

MEDITATION: habituating ourselves to positive attitudes and accurate perspectives.

NIRVANA: the cessation of suffering and its causes. Freedom from cyclic existence.

NOBLE EIGHTFOLD PATH: the path leading to liberation. The eight branches, which can be categorized under the three higher trainings, are correct speech, action, livelihood, mindfulness, concentration, view, realization and effort.

POSITIVE POTENTIAL: imprints of positive actions, which will result in happiness in the future.

PURE LAND: a place established by a Buddha or bodhisattva where all conditions are conducive for practicing Dharma and attaining enlightenment. Pure Land Buddhism is a Mahayana tradition emphasizing methods to be reborn in a pure land.

REALIZATION: a deep understanding that becomes part of us and changes our outlook on the world. When we realize love, for example, the way we feel about and relate to others changes dramatically.

SANGHA: any person who directly and non-conceptually realizes emptiness. In a more general sense, sangha refers to the communities of ordained monks and nuns. It sometimes is used to refer to Buddhists in general.

SELFLESSNESS: see Emptiness.

SPECIAL INSIGHT (VIPASSANA): a wisdom thoroughly discriminating phenomena. It is conjoined with calm abiding and enables one to analyze the meditation object and simultaneously remain single-pointedly on it. This removes ignorance.

SUFFERING (DUKHA): any dissatisfactory condition. It doesn't refer only to physical or mental pain, but includes all problematic conditions.

SUTRA: a teaching of the Buddha; Buddhist scripture. Sutras are found in all Buddhist traditions.

TAKING REFUGE: entrusting one's spiritual development to the guidance of the Buddhas, Dharma and Sangha.

TANTRA: a scripture describing the Vajrayana practice.

THERAVADA: the Tradition of the Elders. This Buddhist tradition is widespread in Southeast Asia and Sri Lanka.

THREE HIGHER TRAININGS: the practices of ethics, meditative concentration and wisdom. Practicing these results in liberation.

THREE JEWELS: the Buddhas, Dharma and Sangha.

THREE PRINCIPAL REALIZATIONS (THREE PRINCIPAL ASPECTS) OF THE PATH: the determination to be free, the altruistic intention and the wisdom realizing emptiness.

VAJRAYANA: a Mahayana Buddhist tradition widespread in Tibet; also known in Japan.

WISDOM REALIZING REALITY: an attitude which correctly understands the manner in which all persons and phenomena exist; i.e., the mind realizing the emptiness of inherent existence.

ZEN (CH'AN): a Mahayana Buddhist tradition widespread in China and Japan.

# Further Reading

Byles, M. B. *Footprints of Gautama Buddha*. Wheaton: Theosophical Publishing House, 1986.

Dhammananda, K. Sri. *How to Live Without Fear and Worry*. Kuala Lumpur: Buddhist Missionary Society, 1989.

Dhammananda, K. Sri. *What Buddhists Believe*. Kuala Lumpur: Buddhist Missionary Society, 1987.

Dhammananda, K. Sri, ed. *The Dhammapada*. Kuala Lumpur: Sasana Abhiwurdhi Wardhana Society, 1988.

Dharmaraksita. *Wheel of Sharp Weapons*. Dharamsala: Library of Tibetan Works and Archives, 1981.

Gampopa. *The Jewel Ornament of Liberation*. Trans. by Herbert Guenther. Boulder: Shambhala, 1971.

Goldstein, Joseph. *The Experience of Insight*. Boston: Shambhala, 1987.

Gyatso, Geshe Kelsang. *Heart of Wisdom*. London: Tharpa, 1986.

H.H. Tenzin Gyatso, the 14th Dalai Lama. *Kindness, Clarity and Insight*. Ithaca: Snow Lion, 1984.

H.H. Tenzin Gyatso, the 14th Dalai Lama. *The Dalai Lama at Harvard*. Trans. by Jeffrey Hopkins. Ithaca: Snow Lion, 1989.

Kapleau, Philip, ed.. *The Three Pillars of Zen*. London: Rider, 1980.

Khema, Ayya. *Being Nobody, Going Nowhere*. Boston: Wisdom, 1987.

216   *Open Heart, Clear Mind*

Kornfield, Jack and Breiter, Paul, eds. *A Still Forest Pool*. Wheaton: Theosophical Publishing House, 1987.

Longchenpa. *Kindly Bent to Ease Us*. Trans. by Herbert Guenther. Emeryville: Dharma Publishing, 1978.

McDonald, Kathleen. *How to Meditate*. Boston: Wisdom, 1984.

Mullin, Glenn, ed. and trans. *Selected Works of the Dalai Lama VII, Songs of Spiritual Change*. Ithaca: Snow Lion, 1982.

Nyanaponika Thera. *Heart of Buddhist Meditation*. London: Rider, 1962.

Nyanaponika Thera. *The Power of Mindfulness*. Kandy: Buddhist Publication Society, 1986.

Rabten, Geshe and Dhargye, Geshe. *Advice from a Spiritual Friend*. Boston: Wisdom, 1986.

Rinpoche, Zopa. *Transforming Problems: Utilizing Happiness and Suffering in the Spiritual Path*. Boston: Wisdom, 1987.

Sparham, Gareth, trans. *Tibetan Dhammapada*. Boston: Wisdom, 1983.

Stevenson, Ian. *Cases of the Reincarnation Type*. 4 vols. Charlottesville: University of Virginia Press, 1975.

Story, Francis. *Rebirth as Doctrine and Experience*. Kandy: Buddhist Publication Society, 1975.

Suzuki, D. T. *An Introduction to Zen Buddhism*. London: Rider, 1969.

Suzuki, Shunriyu. *Zen Mind, Beginner's Mind*. New York: Weatherhill, 1980.

The Third Dalai Lama. *Essence of Refined Gold*. Trans. by Glenn Mullin. Ithaca: Snow Lion, 1985.

Trungpa, Chogyam. *Cutting Through Spiritual Materialism*. London: Shambhala, 1973.

Tsongkhapa, Je. *The Three Principal Aspects of the Path*. Howell, New Jersey: Mahayana Sutra and Tantra Press, 1988.

Wangchen, Geshe. *Awakening the Mind of Enlightenment*. Boston: Wisdom, 1988.

Warder, A. K. *Indian Buddhism*. Delhi: Motilal Banarsidass, 1980.

Yeshe, Lama Thubten. *Introduction to Tantra*. Boston: Wisdom, 1987.

# Dedication

May *Open Heart, Clear Mind* benefit many living beings. May loving-kindness, compassion and a good heart grow within everyone who merely sees, touches or talks about this book. In turn, may they cause many others to develop a kind heart. In this way may everyone enjoy complete satisfaction and peace, and may they ultimately attain enlightenment.

—Ven. Thubten Zopa Rinpoche